Lifelong Learning in the Global Knowledge Economy:
Challenges for Developing Countries

Lifelong Learning in the Global Knowledge Economy:
Challenges for Developing Countries

A World Bank Report

THE WORLD BANK
Washington, D.C.

© 2003 The International Bank for Reconstruction and Development / The World Bank
1818 H Street, NW
Washington, D.C. 20433
Telephone: 202-473-1000
Internet: www.worldbank.org
E-mail: feedback@worldbank.org

ISBN 0-8213-5475-2

Credit for cover photos: World Bank

Library of Congress cataloging-in-publication data has been applied for.

Contents

Figures

Tables

Boxes

Acknowledgments

This study was prepared by a team led by Toby Linden and Harry Anthony Patrinos, who worked under the general direction of Ruth Kagia and the immediate supervision of Jamil Salmi. Team members included David Herbert Fretwell, Kyriakos Georgiades, Richard Hopper, Gwang-Jo Kim, Yoshiko Koda, Kathrin Plangeman, Shobhana Sosale, Masako Uchida, and Ayesha Vawda. Dina Abu-Ghaida, Cecile Fruman, Carolyn Winter, and Mary Eming Young provided additional input. Hernán Araneda, Martin Cristóbal, Pedro Hepp, Yoshiko Koda, Robert L. McGough, Walter McMahon, Hessel Oosterbeek, Miguel Palacios, Denis Ralph, and Frances Tsakonas prepared background papers. The team is grateful for the advice and comments of the peer reviewers: Mary Canning, Barry Chiswick (University of Chicago), Carl Dahlman, Lauritz Holm-Nielsen, Barry McGaw (Organisation for Economic Co-operation and Development), and Alan Wagner (State University of New York, Albany). Hermann-Günter Hesse (German Institute for International Educational Research), Trevor Riordan (International Labour Organization), and Akiko Sakamoto (International Labour Organization) provided useful comments. The team also thanks the people who discussed the document at two review meetings: Sue Berryman, Peter Buckland, Amit Dar, Marito Garcia, Indermit Gill, Thomas Hansen, Yoko Nagashima, Norbert Schady, and especially Aya Aoki, William Experton, Juan Prawda, and Francis Steier, who also provided written comments. The team benefited from discussions of a draft of this report at the international conference "Education—Lifelong Learning and the Knowledge Economy," held in Stuttgart, Germany, in October 2002. Energy James, Inosha Wickramasekera, and especially Micky Ananth and Ma. Lorelei Lacdao helped prepare drafts of the report.

Foreword

The emergence of the global knowledge economy has put a premium on learning throughout the world. Ideas and know-how as sources of economic growth and development, along with the application of new technologies, have important implications for how people learn and apply knowledge throughout their lives.

Lifelong learning is becoming a necessity in many countries. It is more than just education and training beyond formal schooling. A lifelong learning framework encompasses learning throughout the lifecycle, from early childhood to retirement, and in different learning environments, formal, nonformal, and informal. Opportunities for learning throughout one's lifetime are becoming increasingly critical for countries to be competitive in the global knowledge economy.

Lifelong learning is education for the knowledge economy. Within this lifelong learning framework, formal education structures—primary, secondary, higher, vocational, and so on—are less important than learning and meeting learners' needs. It is essential to integrate learning programs better and to align different elements of the system. Learners should be able to enter and leave the system at different points. The learning system needs to include a multitude of players, such as learners, families, employers, providers, and the state. Governance in the lifelong learning framework therefore involves more than just ministries of education and labor.

Consideration of lifelong learning extends the World Bank's traditional approach to education, in which subsectors are examined in isolation. In 1995 *Priorities and Strategies for Education* emphasized the need to look at the education system in a more holistic manner. The 1999 *Education Sector Strategy* discussed the role of new technologies. In 1999, when he articulated the *Comprehensive Development Framework*, World Bank President James Wolfensohn referred explicitly to lifelong learning as a part of what education means for poverty alleviation. In 2002 the World Bank completed important new policy work on tertiary (higher) education reforms as well as a vision paper on the role of science and technology. This report represents the Bank's first attempt to lay out an analytical framework for understanding the challenges of developing a lifelong learning system.

The World Bank's involvement in lifelong learning is still at the conceptual stage, but two new projects—in Romania and Chile—have already been prepared to address the need for continuing education and lifelong learning. In the years to come we expect to conduct more analytical work on lifelong learning, and the policy dialogue in education will touch more and more on lifelong learning issues. Our lending program will undoubtedly involve operations to support countries' efforts to transform their education systems to reflect a lifelong learning approach. This report provides a departure point for these continuing discussions.

Ruth Kagia
Director, Education
Human Development Network
World Bank

Preface

This report explores the challenges to education and training systems that the knowledge economy presents. It outlines policy options for addressing these challenges and developing viable systems of lifelong learning in developing countries and countries with transition economies. It addresses four questions:

- What does a national education and training system, including its formal and nonformal components, need to do to support knowledge-based economic growth?
- How can developing countries and countries with transition economies promote lifelong learning, and what challenges do they face in doing so?
- Given limited resources, what type of governance framework promotes lifelong learning for people in general and disadvantaged groups in particular?
- How can financing of lifelong learning be inclusive, affordable, and sustainable?

The report provides a conceptual framework for education-related lending activities reflecting the latest knowledge and successful practices of planning and implementing education for lifelong learning. It encourages countries to look beyond traditional approaches to education and training and to engage in a policy dialogue on the pedagogical and economic consequences of lifelong learning.

This is a consultative document, on which the World Bank welcomes comments. Readers should send their comments to the Education Advisory Service, 1818 H Street, NW, Washington, D.C., 20433, United States, or e-mail them to eservice@worldbank.org. The World Bank hopes that this report will encourage discussion within developing countries and countries with transition economies.

Executive Summary

A knowledge-based economy relies primarily on the use of ideas rather than physical abilities and on the application of technology rather than the transformation of raw materials or the exploitation of cheap labor. Knowledge is being developed and applied in new ways. Product cycles are shorter and the need for innovation greater. Trade is expanding worldwide, increasing competitive demands on producers.

The global knowledge economy is transforming the demands of the labor market throughout the world. It is also placing new demands on citizens, who need more skills and knowledge to be able to function in their day-to-day lives.

Equipping people to deal with these demands requires a new model of education and training, a model of lifelong learning. A lifelong learning framework encompasses learning throughout the lifecycle, from early childhood through retirement. It encompasses formal learning (schools, training institutions, universities); nonformal learning (structured on-the-job training); and informal learning (skills learned from family members or people in the community). It allows people to access learning opportunities as they need them rather than because they have reached a certain age.

Lifelong learning is crucial to preparing workers to compete in the global economy. But it is important for other reasons as well. By improving people's ability to function as members of their communities, education and training increase social cohesion, reduce crime, and improve income distribution.

Developing countries and countries with transition economies risk being further marginalized in a competitive global knowledge economy because their education and training systems are not equipping learners with the skills they need. To respond to the problem, policymakers need to make fundamental changes. They need to replace the information-based, teacher-directed rote learning provided within a formal education system governed by directives with a new type of learning that emphasizes creating, applying, analyzing, and synthesizing knowledge and engaging in collaborative learning throughout the lifespan. This report describes several ways this can be done.

Creating a Labor Force Able to Compete in the Global Economy

In traditional industries most jobs require employees to learn how to perform routine functions, which, for the most part, remain constant over time. Most learning takes place when a worker starts a new job. In the knowledge economy, change is so rapid that workers constantly need to acquire new skills. Firms can no longer rely solely on new graduates or new labor market entrants as the primary source of new skills and knowledge. Instead, they need workers who are willing and able to update their skills throughout their lifetimes. Countries need to respond to these needs by creating education and training systems that equip people with the appropriate skills.

The private sector is playing a growing role
in education throughout the world

Traditionally, the public sector provided most education services. Today that is changing. In many middle-income countries, the private education sector is growing, fostered by the poor quality and coverage of public education and the need to relieve fiscal burdens and promote innovation. Since 1995 the number of students enrolled in higher education in Brazil has grown more than 70 percent, with most of this increase occurring in private colleges and universities, which now account for 71 percent of higher education enrollment. In China 500 new institutions of higher learning were established between 1995 and 1999.

The private education sector is growing rapidly in countries with transition economies as well. Poland alone has 195 private higher education institutions, which educate more than 377,000 students. Private business schools—unheard of in Eastern Europe 10 years ago—are also thriving: in 1998 there were 91 private business schools in Poland, 29 in the Czech Republic, 18 in Romania, and 4 in Bulgaria.

At the same time, new providers—private sector trainers, virtual universities, international providers, corporate universities, educational publishers, content brokers, and media companies—have arisen to complement and challenge traditional institutions. This growth of the private sector reflects the rising demand for more and better education as well as dissatisfaction with the traditional education and training system.

Spending on training has increased dramatically

Corporations are spending more and more on training to become or remain competitive in the global knowledge economy. Worldwide, annual corporate training expenditures reached $28 billion in 2002, up from $18 billion in 1997.

Transforming Learning to Meet Learners' Lifelong Needs

Being successful in the knowledge economy requires mastering a new set of knowledge and competencies. These include basic academic skills, such as literacy, foreign language, math, and science skills, and the ability to use information and communication technology. Workers must be able to use these skills effectively, act autonomously and reflectively, and join and function in socially heterogeneous groups.

Many countries have not been successful in providing people with knowledge and competencies

Education is inadequate in most developing countries. Coverage is insufficient, access is inequitable (especially in tertiary education and in employee and adult training), and the quality of education is poor. Adult literacy rates are low, and too few children complete basic education. International assessments of secondary school students in math and science show countries with developing and transition economies trailing significantly, especially when students are tested on their ability to apply and use knowledge.

In the transition economies of Europe and Central Asia, the quality of education is inadequate and the education system is too rigid. Rote learning, exam-driven schooling, and the soaring cost of private education have long been policy concerns in some Asian countries.

Traditional education methods are ill suited to providing people with the skills they need

The traditional learning model differs from lifelong learning methods in important ways:

Traditional learning	Lifelong learning
• The teacher is the source of knowledge.	• Educators are guides to sources of knowledge.
• Learners receive knowledge from the teacher.	• People learn by doing.
• Learners work by themselves.	• People learn in groups and from one another.
• Tests are given to prevent progress until students have completely mastered a set of skills and to ration access to further learning.	• Assessment is used to guide learning strategies and identify pathways for future learning.
• All learners do the same thing.	• Educators develop individualized learning plans.
• Teachers receive initial training plus ad hoc in-service training.	• Educators are lifelong learners. Initial training and ongoing professional development are linked.
• "Good" learners are identified and permitted to continue their education.	• People have access to learning opportunities over a lifetime.

Teacher training needs to change

This new learning context implies a different role for teachers and trainers. Teachers need to learn new skills and become lifelong learners themselves to keep up to date with new knowledge, pedagogical ideas, and technology. As learning becomes more collaborative, so too must teachers' professional development, which needs to promote professional networks and learning organizations within schools and institutions.

ICTs can support changes in pedagogy and teacher training—given the appropriate policy framework

Information and communication technologies (ICTs) can facilitate learning by doing (through computer simulations, for example). They can vastly increase the information resources available to learners, thereby changing the relationship between teacher and student. They can facilitate collaborative learning and provide rapid feedback to learners.

These outcomes do not emerge simply through the introduction of computers into the learning setting, however. An appropriate policy framework is needed in which ICTs are used to tackle educational problems; significant investment is made in training teachers and managers to change their knowledge and behavior; qualified technicians and support staff are available; and funding for maintenance, access to the Internet, and upgrading is sustainable. These conditions are rarely met, especially in developing countries.

Formal education institutions need to become more flexible

An increasing number of tertiary institutions are offering part-time, evening, weekend, and summer courses to meet the needs of working adults. In Finland the number of adults enrolled in continuing education programs at the tertiary level exceeds the number of young people enrolled in traditional degree courses.

Distance education is one way in which countries can offer more flexible learning opportunities. Many countries use interactive radio instruction in basic education. Mexico uses television to educate about 15 percent of its lower secondary school students. In the 1990s the National Teachers Institute in Nigeria graduated more teachers through its distance learning program than all other programs in the country combined. The Internet is beginning to transform higher education and corporate training. In 1999, for example, 92 percent of large corporations in the United States piloted Web-based training programs.

Governing a Lifelong Learning System

To create effective lifelong learning systems, countries need to make significant changes to both the governance and the financing of education and training. In many industrial countries, governments that once focused exclusively on public financing and public provision of education and training are now trying to create flexible policy and regulatory frameworks that encompass a wider range of institutional actors. These frameworks include legislation and executive orders; arrangements for ensuring coordination across ministries and other institutions involved in education and training activities; and mechanisms for certifying the achievements of learners, monitoring institutional and system performance, and promoting learning pathways. Within this framework, the role of incentives is critical.

The public sector can no longer be the sole provider of education

The state will have to increase its cooperation with the private sector and civil society. The private sector can provide education in both traditional ways (owning and operating private schools and providing inputs, such as books, materials, and equipment) and novel ways (operating public schools under contract). Enterprises also provide training and are increasingly involved in developing occupational standards and curricula.

Government ministries need to coordinate their activities

Agreements and ongoing collaboration among central, regional, and local governments in implementation are needed. In some countries, including Germany and the Republic of Korea, coordination has been promoted by merging the departments responsible for education and training. In contrast, in many developing countries many ministries, including industry-specific ministries, oversee, manage, and finance training. Competition for scarce resources in these countries prevents collaboration, promotion of high-quality training, and development of a continuum of training opportunities.

Quality assurance systems are needed to assess learners and inform them about providers

The outcomes of learning must be monitored effectively. Quality assurance systems need to recognize the range of formal and informal settings in which learning takes place, and they need to provide opportunities for learners to demonstrate their newly acquired skills and knowledge. Quality assurance systems also need to provide prospective learners with information about the offerings and performance of providers.

Quality assurance systems can also make it easier for learners to move among different types and levels of learning environments. Namibia, New Zealand, South Africa, and the United Kingdom have national qualification systems, which assign qualifications from different institutions to a set of levels, each linked to competency standards. Students at colleges and universities in the United States can transfer credits from one institution to another. And Europe-wide agreement on equivalences and quality assurance mechanisms is emerging (through the Bologna process).

Policymakers need to rethink accreditation of institutions

Some industrial and developing countries are beginning to accredit institutions on the basis of output or performance measures (such as graduation rates) rather than on the basis of input measures (such as the number of books in the library or faculty). In Bangladesh, for example, private secondary schools are supposed to achieve certain pass rates on the university entrance examination to remain accredited (although the regulation is rarely enforced). In Armenia a certain percentage of students (currently 50 percent) at private (but not public) higher education institutions must pass the final examination. Increasingly, funding of institutions is also based on performance.

Financing Lifelong Learning

More and higher-quality education and training opportunities over a lifetime will require increased expenditures, although resources will also need to be used more efficiently and in different ways. These expenditures cannot be met solely from public sources. What is needed is a menu of sustainable and equitable options that combine public and private financing.

*The private and public sectors need
to work together to finance learning*

Governments need to finance lifelong learning for which social returns exceed private returns (for example, basic education). The private sector needs to play a role in financing investments for which private returns are high (for example, most higher and continuing education). Government intervention beyond the basic skills and knowledge should be targeted to learners from low-income or socially excluded groups and others facing high barriers to learning.

*No single financing system can
serve the needs of all learners*

Policymakers need to consider a range of financing options, including subsidies, mortgage-type loans, human capital contracts, graduate taxes, income-contingent repayment schemes, entitlement schemes, asset-building schemes, and individual learning accounts. Whatever mechanisms are used, financing of learning beyond the basic competencies should include both cost-sharing and subsidy components. Subsidies could be the main source of financing for low-income learners. For higher-income groups, most financing could take the form of income-contingent loans at market interest rates.

Agenda for the Future

The demands of a lifelong learning system are enormous, and most countries will not be able to implement all elements of the system at once. Countries must therefore develop a strategy for moving forward in a systematic and sequenced fashion. An important step is to identify where a country stands, particularly with respect to its international peers.

National systems of lifelong learning need to be benchmarked

One way in which countries could move forward would be by establishing national benchmarks for measuring lifelong learning outcomes. Such measures are underdeveloped. Traditional measures of educational progress, such as gross enrollment ratios and public spending as a proportion of GDP, do not capture important dimensions of lifelong learning. Gross enrollment ratios measure inputs rather than achievement of core or other competencies. Total education spending includes more than just public spending. Traditional indicators also fail to capture learning in the non-formal and informal sectors, which is becoming increasingly important.

A different approach to education reform is needed

Continual reform is needed not only to accelerate the pace of reform but also to deepen the extent to which fundamental transformation of learning is carried out. The traditional model of education reform, however, is not amenable to constant change: streams of initiatives and policy changes are viewed as overwhelming to education stakeholders, causing reform fatigue and resistance to set in. Reform and change must therefore be built into institutions' own processes. In addition, policy changes need broad support and dialogue to facilitate ongoing adjustments during implementation.

The World Bank will continue to deepen its understanding and help countries develop concrete strategies

National policymakers and stakeholders worldwide need to engage in a dialogue on lifelong learning, helping governments formulate visions and concrete action plans for establishing both lifelong learning and innovation frameworks appropriate to their country contexts. The World Bank can help in this effort by deepening the understanding of the implications of the knowledge economy for education and training systems and by disseminating analytical and policy documents on education for the knowledge economy.

Acronyms and Abbreviations

ESA	education savings account
IALS	International Adult Literacy Survey
ICTs	information and communication technologies
ILA	individual learning account
IRI	Interactive Radio Instruction
MIT	Massachusetts Institute of Technology
OECD	Organisation for Economic Co-operation and Development
PDA	personal development account
PISA	Programme for International Student Assessment
TIMSS	Third International Mathematics and Science Study

1
The Knowledge Economy and the Changing Needs of the Labor Market

Knowledge is our most powerful engine of production.

Alfred Marshall, 1890

All agree that the single most important key to development and to poverty allevi-ation is education. This must start with universal primary education for girls and boys equally, as well as an open and competitive system of secondary and tertiary education . . . . Adult education, literacy, and lifelong learning must be combined with the fundamental recognition that education of women and girls is central to the process of development.

James D. Wolfensohn, President of the World Bank, 1999

A knowledge-based economy relies primarily on the use of ideas rather than physical abilities and on the application of technology rather than the transformation of raw materials or the exploitation of cheap labor. It is an economy in which knowledge is created, acquired, transmitted, and used more effectively by individuals, enterprises, organizations, and com-munities to promote economic and social development (World Bank Insti-tute 2001c; World Bank 1998d). Knowledge can either be codified and written down or tacit and in people's heads.

The knowledge economy is transforming the demands of the labor market in economies throughout the world. In industrial countries, where knowledge-based industries are expanding rapidly, labor market demands are changing accordingly. Where new technologies have been introduced, demand for high-skilled workers, particularly high-skilled information and communication technology (ICT) workers, has increased. At the same time, demand for lower-skilled workers has declined (OECD 2001f).

1

Four features of the knowledge economy have far-ranging implications for education and training:

- *Knowledge is being developed and applied in new ways.* The information revolution has expanded networks and provided new opportunities for access to information. It has also created new opportunities for generating and transferring information. Knowledge networks and sharing of information have expedited innovation and adaptation capacity. Changes in ICT have revolutionized the transmission of information. Semiconductors are getting faster, computer memories are expanding, and ICT prices are falling. Data transmission costs have fallen dramatically and continue to fall, bandwidth is growing, and Internet hosts are expanding and multiplying. Cellular phone usage is growing worldwide, adding to the pace of and capacity for change and innovation.
- *Product cycles are shorter and the need for innovation greater.* In 1990 it took six years to go from concept to production in the automobile industry; today that process takes just two years. The number of patent applications is growing, and more and more international and multiple applications are being filed. Industrial countries filed 82,846 patent applications at the European Patent Office in 1997, a 37 percent increase over 1990 (OECD 2001f).
- *Trade is increasing worldwide, increasing competitive demands on producers.* Countries that are able to integrate into the world economy may be able to achieve higher economic growth and improve health and education outcomes (World Bank 2002e).
- *Small and medium-size enterprises in the service sector have become increasingly important players, in terms of both economic growth and employment.*

A knowledge economy rests on four pillars (World Bank Institute 2001c):

- A supportive economic and institutional regime to provide incentives for the efficient use of existing and new knowledge and the flourishing of entrepreneurship.
- An educated and skilled population to create, share, and use knowledge.
- A dynamic information infrastructure to facilitate the effective communication, dissemination, and processing of information.
- An efficient innovation system of firms, research centers, universities, consultants, and other organizations to tap into the growing stock of global knowledge, assimilate and adapt it to local needs, and create new technology.

This chapter focuses on the role of education and training in helping build the second and fourth pillars of a knowledge economy.

Implications of the Knowledge Economy for Education and Training

Preparing workers to compete in the knowledge economy requires a new model of education and training, a model of lifelong learning. A lifelong learning framework encompasses learning throughout the life cycle, from early childhood to retirement. It includes formal, nonformal, and informal education and training.

- Formal education and training includes structured programs that are recognized by the formal education system and lead to approved certificates.
- Nonformal education and training includes structured programs that are not formally recognized by the national system. Examples include apprenticeship training programs and structured on-the-job training.
- Informal education and training includes unstructured learning, which can take place almost anywhere, including the home, community, or workplace. It includes unstructured on-the-job training, the most common form of workplace learning.

Recent knowledge and the accumulated stock of human capital are inputs in the production of new knowledge and wealth. The speed of change in the knowledge economy means that skills depreciate much more rapidly than they once did. To compete effectively in this constantly changing environment, workers need to be able to upgrade their skills on a continuing basis.

Change in the knowledge economy is so rapid that firms can no longer rely solely on new graduates or new labor market entrants as the primary source of new skills and knowledge. Schools and other training institutions thus need to prepare workers for lifelong learning. Educational systems can no longer emphasize task-specific skills but must focus instead on developing learners' decisionmaking and problem-solving skills and teaching them how to learn on their own and with others.

Lifelong learning is crucial in enabling workers to compete in the global economy. Education helps reduce poverty; if developing countries do not promote lifelong learning opportunities, the skills and technology gap between them and industrial countries will continue to grow. By improving people's ability to function as members of their communities, education and training also increase social capital (broadly defined as social cohesion or social ties), thereby helping to build human capital, increase economic growth, and stimulate development. Social capital also improves education and health outcomes and child welfare, increases tolerance for gender and racial equity, enhances civil liberty and economic and civic equity, and decreases crime and tax evasion (Putnam 2001). Education must thus be viewed as fundamental to development, not just because it enhances human capital but because it increases social capital as well.

Human Capital and Knowledge as Sources of Economic Growth

Investment in human capital is critical for economic growth. Particularly important are new technology, its dissemination through education, and related externalities (Romer 1989; Lucas 1988; Barro 1991; Mankiw, Romer, and Weil 1992). Researchers have documented the external effects of human capital in Austria, China, and Guatemala (Winter-Ebmer 1994; Wang and Mody 1997; Sakellariou 2001). They have tied growth to knowledge in Israel and found significant spillover effects of human capital in the Republic of Korea (Bregman and Marom 1993; Feenstra and others 1999).

Technology and economic growth are strongly correlated in industrial countries. Computer hardware was linked strongly to output growth in the late 1990s, when it is estimated to have contributed as much as 2.5 percent to increases in output (table 1.1).

Table 1.1. Contribution of Computer Hardware to Output Growth, 1990–99 (percent)

Country	Period	Contribution to output growth	Period	Contribution to output growth
Australia	1990–95	0.31	1995–99	0.57
Canada	1990–96	0.28	1995–99	0.36
Germany	1990–96	0.19	1995–99	0.14
Finland	1990–95	0.00	1995–99	0.11
France	1990–95	0.00	1996–99	0.10
Italy	1990–96	0.21	1995–99	0.12
Japan	1990–96	0.19	1995–99	0.29
Singapore	–	–	1977–97	1.50
Korea, Rep. of	–	–	1980–95	2.50
United Kingdom	1990–95	0.10	1996–99	0.30
United States	1990–95	0.33	1996–98	0.82

– Not available.

Source: Original sources cited in Patrinos 2001a.

The link between education and economic growth strengthens as the rate of technology transfer increases (Sab and Smith 2001). The fact that an impact on growth is observed only in more affluent countries, where the overall level of education is higher, suggests that technology adoption is strongly linked to the education of the labor force (Pohjola 2000).

The threshold level of human capital accumulation beyond which a country may experience accelerating growth is estimated at a literacy rate of 40 percent (Azariadis and Drazen 1990). Once countries reach this threshold, they can increase growth by opening their economies to technology transfer, as Costa Rica has done (box 1.1).

The impact of education on economic growth may be as high as the private returns to education estimated in microeconomic studies (see Krueger and Lindahl 1999; Topel 1999). Estimates suggest that changes in educational attainment—as opposed to the initial level of education used in most of the macroeconomic growth literature—affect cross-country income growth at least as much as they affect microeconomic estimates of the private rate of return to years of schooling. Typically, an additional year of schooling raises incomes 10 percent; in very poor countries it can increase incomes 20 percent or more (Psacharopoulos and Patrinos 2002). Data on within-country changes in education and productivity suggest that a one-year increase in average years of schooling for a country's labor force raises output per worker 5–15 percent (Topel 1999).

The quality of education, and therefore of labor, also affects economic growth (Barro 2001; Hanushek and Kimko 2000). Science achievement, for example, has a positive effect on growth.

Box 1.1. Why Did Intel Choose Costa Rica as the Site of a Multimillion Dollar Plant?

In 1996 Costa Rica beat out Brazil, Chile, Indonesia, Mexico, the Philippines, and Thailand to become the site of Intel's $300 million semiconductor assembly and test plant. Many factors made Costa Rica attractive to Intel—its stable economic and political system, its liberalized economy, a growing electronics sector, and incentives and tax breaks—but the crucial factor in securing its selection was its educated labor force.

Since 1948, when democracy was restored, Costa Rica has placed strong emphasis on education, adopting a demand-driven approach. The government invested heavily in education and technology training, and it adopted a bilingual ESL (English as Second Language) curriculum. Computers were introduced into elementary schools as early as 1988; by 1996 many schools were equipped with them.

Source: World Bank 1998a, 2001f.

Technological progress is likely to raise the value of education in producing human capital (Schultz 1975). As developing countries liberalize their trade regimes and open themselves to technology transfer from industrial countries, the value of education rises. Education thus becomes more important.

Of course, the impact of education varies by country; without appropriate incentives high returns will not materialize (Pritchett 2001; Wolff 2000). As discussed in chapter 2, the quality of education is important. The productivity of schooling may be much lower in countries where the government does not promote an environment favorable to the creation of higher-paying jobs and a significant number of educated workers work in the public sector (Pissarides 2000; see also Gundlach 2001). Policies that artificially compress wage differentials also reduce the returns to post-schooling investment. This is particularly true in Sub-Saharan Africa and the Middle East and North Africa, less so in Latin America and Asia.

The literature establishes that education matters, but it does not describe the channels through which it affects growth. Large indirect effects of education, operating through intervening variables, raise the social rates of return significantly, sometimes with long delays. The size of these effects is not clear, however, with some estimates yielding negative and others yielding very high positive values (table 1.2). A study of Uganda found that a one-year increase in the average number of years of primary schooling of neighboring farmers was associated with a

Table 1.2. Evidence on Human Capital Externalities (percent)

Source	Social return	Private return
Cross-country Mincer regressions		
Benhabib and Spiegel 1994	3.9	–
Benhabib and Spiegel 1994	Negative	–
Heckman and Klenow 1997	23.0	6–10
Heckman and Klenow 1997	10.6	–
Topel 1999	22.6	–
Topel 1999	6.2	–
Micro studies		
Rauch 1993 (United States)	8.1	4.8
Acemoglou and Angrist 1999 (United States)	14.6	7.3
Acemoglou and Angrist 1999 (United States)	9.1	7.4
Rural farmer studies		
Appleton and Balihuta 1996 (Uganda)	4.3	2.8
Weir 1999 (Ethiopia)	56.0	2.0

– Not available.
Sources: Venniker 2000; Appleton 2000.

4.3 percent rise in output—a larger increase than the 2.8 percent effect of an increase in the farmer's own education (Appleton and Balihuta 1996). The indirect feedback effects on per capita economic growth are estimated at about 93 percent of the total effects (direct and indirect) for the composite Sub-Saharan Africa average (Appiah and McMahon 2002). In the more advanced African countries, indirect feedback effects account for about 48 percent of the total.

Education also has an important effect on several nonmarket outcomes, including crime reduction, social cohesion, income distribution, charitable giving, and more efficient labor market search. The annual value of one year of schooling on these outcomes is about the same as the annual earnings-based effects. That is, the value of incremental schooling reported in standard human capital estimates may capture only about half of the total value of an additional year of schooling (Wolfe and Haveman 2001).

Education has an important effect on female productivity in the labor market. Even more important are the positive effects on female labor supply; the associated declines in fertility; and the improvements in the health, education, and life chances of the children of educated women. There is a strong linkage between mothers' education and children's development. In India, for example, children raised by literate mothers are more likely to study two additional hours a day than children of illiterate mothers (World Bank 2001f). These findings have important implications for economic growth and lifelong learning from an intergenerational perspective.

The State of Education in Developing Countries and Transition Economies

Education is inadequate in most developing countries. Coverage is insufficient, access is inequitable (especially in tertiary [higher] education and in employee and adult training), and the quality of education is poor. Adult literacy rates are low, and too few children complete basic education. The goal of education for all remains elusive in many low-income countries.

In the transition economies of Europe and Central Asia, the quality of education is inadequate and the education system is too rigid. Rote learning, exam-driven schooling, and the soaring cost of private education have long been policy concerns in some Asian countries.

Evidence from international assessments of students suggests that some developing countries and transition economies lag significantly behind industrial countries in providing their people with the skills needed in the knowledge economy (see chapter 2). Policy actions are needed to reduce inequities in the distribution of learning opportunities and discrepancies in the incidence of the costs and benefits of education.

Developing countries and transition economies face the dual challenge of addressing the longstanding issues of access, quality, and equity while moving toward a lifelong learning system. Basic education and skills remain the foundation of lifelong learning, and countries with low or declining basic education coverage must set increasing coverage as their top priority. The quality and nature of the learning process must change, however, and outcomes must improve.

Increased Demand for Skills

Increasing returns to schooling and rising wage inequality are well documented for some industrial countries and a few developing countries in the 1980s and 1990s. These changes partly reflect the important technological developments that took place during this time.

Rising Returns to Schooling

A reversal of the 1970s trend of declining rewards to higher education and falling rates of return to schooling occurred in the United States and other industrial market economies in the 1980s and 1990s. The gap in wages between educated and less educated workers widened significantly during the 1980s (table 1.3). Between 1978 and 1987 the rate of return to edu-

Table 1.3. Value of Higher Education in Industrial Countries, 1970s–1990s

Decade	Country	Year	Wage ratio (higher/secondary)	Year	Wage ratio (higher/secondary)
1970s	Canada	1970	1.65	1980	1.40
	Sweden	1968	1.40	1981	1.16
	United Kingdom	1974	1.64	1980	1.53
	United States	1969	1.49	1978	1.35
1980s	Canada	1980	1.29	1989	1.35
	Sweden	1981	1.16	1986	1.19
	United Kingdom	1980	1.33	1989	1.46
	United States	1979	1.47	1987	1.52
1990s	Canada	1992	1.62	1997	1.48
	Sweden	1992	1.60	1998	1.36
	United Kingdom	1992	1.71	1999	1.59
	United States	1992	1.64	1999	1.83

Sources: Patrinos 2001a; OECD 1992, 2001b.

cation for male workers in the United States rose from 7.9 percent to 9.2 percent, and the average number of years of schooling increased from 12.6 to 13.3 years (Ryscavage and Henle 1990).

Increasing wage disparity was particularly severe in the rapidly expanding service sector, where the decline in the variance in schooling was most dramatic. Ryscavage and Henle (1990) found that among white-collar workers classified as administrators, officials, and sales workers, more educated workers increased their earnings advantage over less educated workers. The wages of educated workers in traded services increased the most, while goods industries that were declining, such as manufacturing, experienced decreases in output, employment, and wages (Murphy and Welch 1991).

The decline in earnings differentials in the mid- to late 1990s suggests that the supply of education caught up with demand. It is noteworthy, however, that in the industrial country with the highest growth during this period, the United States, the demand for educated labor resulted in an increase in earnings differentials between those with higher education and those with only secondary education.

In most lower-income countries for which comparable data are available, the returns to primary schooling have declined with the expansion of the supply of education. This is not to say that the returns to schooling are low. On the contrary, returns to schooling are highest in lower-income countries (figure 1.1). As universal primary education is achieved, shortages of skills in the labor force occur more at the junior and senior secondary levels, and the relative returns to these levels of education rise.

Figure 1.1. Private Returns to Investment in Education, by Level of Education and Country Income Group (percent)

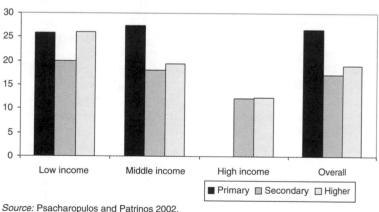

Source: Psacharopulos and Patrinos 2002.

Table 1.4. Higher/Secondary Education Earnings Ratios in Middle-Income Countries, 1980s–1990s

Country	1981 (or nearest year) Ratio	1981 (or nearest year) Years of schooling[a]	1989 Ratio	1989 Years of schooling[b]	1995 (or nearest year) Ratio	1995 (or nearest year) Years of schooling	1999 Ratio	1999 Years of schooling[c]
Argentina	2.44	6.62	1.71	7.77	1.66	8.12	2.03	8.49
Brazil	2.30	2.98	2.01	3.76	2.59	4.17	2.70	4.56
Chile	–	–	–	–	2.96	7.53	2.79	7.89
Czech Rep.	–	–	1.29	9.39	1.63	9.38	–	–
Greece	1.62	6.56	1.25	6.95	1.28	8.05	–	–
Uruguay	1.54	5.75	1.54	6.69	1.88	6.88	1.96	7.25
Venezuela	1.82	4.93	1.72	4.89	1.82	5.48	–	–

– Not available.

Note: Ratio = earnings of learners with higher education over earnings of learners with secondary education.

a. Data are for 1980.

b. Data are for 1990.

c. Data are for 2000.

Sources: Patrinos 2001a; Carlson 2001; Klazar, Sedmihradsky, and Vancurova 2001; World Bank 1998g. Years of schooling are from Barro and Lee 2000.

Later, as universal secondary education is nearly achieved, relative short-ages occur for people with still more advanced skills, and the rates of return to two- and four-year college degrees are highest.

In middle-income countries, the earnings ratio appeared to trend downward in the few countries for which 1980s data are available (table 1.4). By the 1990s, however, the trend was clearly upward in the Czech Republic, Greece, and the middle-income Latin American countries.

Between 1980 and 2000 the proportion of the population with higher education rose from 7 to 20 percent in Argentina, from 5 to 8 percent in Brazil, from 7 to 16 percent in Chile, from 9 to 11 percent in the Czech Republic, from 8 to 14 percent in Greece, from 8 to 13 percent in Uruguay, and from 7 to 18 percent in Venezuela (Barro and Lee 2000). Returns to schooling increased in Mexico for higher levels of schooling, particularly university-level education. In Brazil returns to higher education rose from 16 percent in 1982 to 20 percent in 1988 (figure 1.2). This evidence suggests that there is increased demand for highly skilled labor, especially in countries with open markets.

The relative supply of skilled labor increased at the same time that trade liberalization in Chile, Colombia, Costa Rica, Mexico, and Uruguay increased demand for partly skilled labor more than demand for unskilled labor (Robbins 1996; World Bank 2002h). This suggests that labor demand in these countries has shifted toward workers with above-average skill

Figure 1.2. Returns to Schooling in Brazil, 1982 and 1998

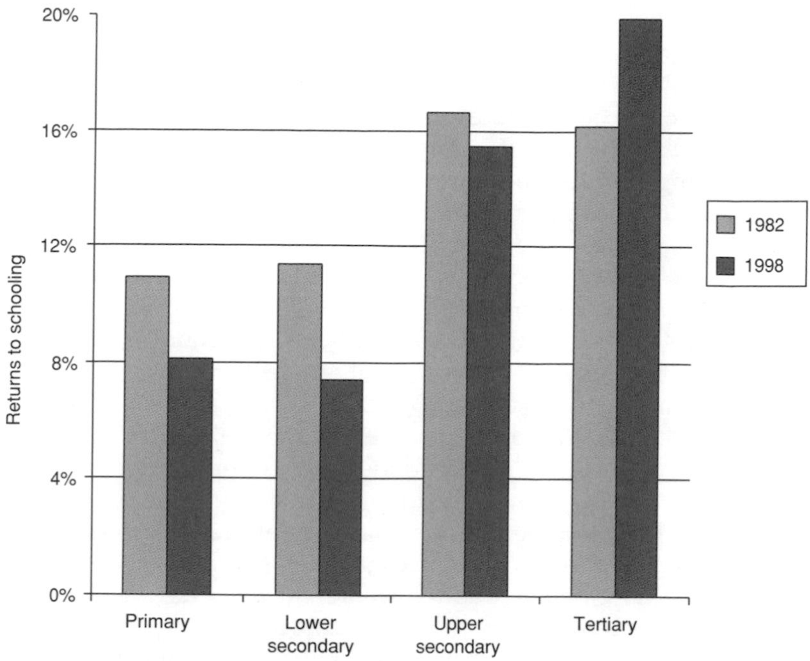

Source: Blom, Holm-Nielsen, and Verner 2001.

levels, thereby increasing income inequality (Slaughter and Swagel 1997). In Mexico and Venezuela a higher level of foreign investment in an industry—often one employing better-educated workers—is associated with higher wages in that industry, also contributing to rising inequality (Aitken, Harrison, and Lipsey 1996). In Poland wages and growth rates are higher in industries with greater foreign presence (Bedi and Cieoelik 2002). In transition economies the longer the reform process—and therefore the longer market forces, openness, and foreign investment have been allowed to operate—the higher the premium to education over time (World Bank 2002e).

If the incomes of more educated workers continue to rise despite an increase in their numbers, demand for these workers can be assumed to have risen more than supply. If increases in demand continue to outstrip increases in supply, returns to schooling (and income inequality) will continue to increase (Psacharopoulos 1989; Tinbergen 1975; see also Welch 1970). The relationship can be viewed as a "race between education and technology" (Tinbergen 1975).

Technological Change and the Demand for Skilled Labor

The rise in earnings inequality can be explained by changes in technology, the production process, work organization, and patterns of international trade (Wood 1994). Changes in the production process led to changes in the demand for certain types of labor. Organizational and technological changes may have caused the shift in demand to dominate the shift in supply, leading to a rise in returns to schooling and increased earnings inequality in advanced economies and some middle-income countries.

In Malaysia widespread adoption of ICTs has been associated with wage and productivity gains (Tan 2000). Significant "learning effects" occur with experience using ICTs, and productivity gains increase with training (Berman and Machin 2000). Skill-biased technology transfer is central to the increased demand for skilled workers in middle-income countries (Berman and Machin 2000).

Education supports innovation and helps speed the diffusion of technology. It not only facilitates learning and communication but also increases substantially the ability to deal creatively with change. Educated workers have a comparative advantage with respect to adjustment to, and implementation of, new technologies (Bartel and Lichtenberg 1987, 1988). Because better-educated workers usually have a broader set of basic skills, it is easier for them to assimilate new knowledge, and their earnings rise more quickly than those with lower educational levels (box 1.2). Better-educated people are also better able to deal with economic

---

Box 1.2. Technological and Organizational Change: A Case Study of a Commercial Bank in the United States

Technological change can have vastly different effects, even on departments within the same institution. The same technological change can result in both computer-labor substitution and computer-skill complementarity (skill-biased technological change), depending on the nature of work and the organization of the workplace. Technological change and organizational change are interdependent. Conceptual and problem-solving skills are one set of skills that are likely to be made more valuable by ICTs. To examine how computer technology complements skilled labor, the study looked at what computers do to model and test how computers alter the demand for skilled labor. It found that computers are associated with declining relative demand in the industry for routine skills and increased demand for nonroutine cognitive skills.

Source: Autor, Levy, and Murnane 2002.

disequilibria (Schultz 1975). Firms undergoing rapid technological change want to employ better-educated and more talented workers, in whom they are also more willing to invest in training and retraining. Thus the more volatile the state of technology, the more productive education is (Nelson and Phelps 1966; Welch 1970).

Migration

Another indicator of the premium to human capital is migration of people from their home countries to countries in which their skills, and the benefits of their educational investment, are more highly rewarded. About 120 million people (2 percent of the world's population) live in countries in which they were not born (most of these immigrants are lower-skilled workers). The main economic rationale for moving is higher wages and greater employment opportunities. Migration, which is costly in terms of time and out-of-pocket expenditures, represents a form of human capital. It is a powerful means of raising incomes and promoting the diffusion of knowledge. From a global perspective, economic welfare is increased if people are more productive abroad than they would have been in their home country (box 1.3). Migrants thus increase world welfare, including in the country they left.

In the short term, migration, especially the migration of highly skilled people, can hurt the source country. The loss of people who provide vital public services—doctors, information technology specialists, teachers—can retard low-income countries' development, even if the number of such emigrants is small. Migration may prevent the source country from being able to reach the critical mass of human capital that may spark innovations, in entrepreneurship or knowledge creation, adaptation, and

---

Box 1.3. Impact of Migration of Technology Graduates from India

About 40 percent of India's technology graduates leave the country and do not return. In 1998 Indian engineers were running more than 775 technology companies in California's Silicon Valley—companies that together billed $3.6 billion in sales and employed 16,600 people. About 40 percent of Silicon Valley start-ups were established by Indians.

Although many Indians never return to their native country, most eventually invest in India and contribute to the development of the local information technology industry. Many Indian expatriates invest in Bangalore, in southern India, the Silicon Valley of India. Other benefits include remittances and investments in homes.

Source: World Bank 2001b.

use. A migrant may increase the supply of goods and services only to already wealthy inhabitants of the recipient country. The higher salary earned by a doctor, for example, may reflect the greater ability of rich people to pay for medical services. Given funding sources, the creativity of highly skilled researchers may be used to conduct research on problems that are of primary concern to the industrial world rather than their home countries.

Migration pressures will continue to mount in developing countries, especially for highly skilled workers, as countries trade more openly. Industrial countries could help ease these pressures by opening their doors to the less skilled as well as to highly skilled migrants (World Bank 2002e).

Source countries could help by adopting economic and other policies that make effective use of human capital in both public and private sectors and motivate migrants to return. These policies, which need to differentiate between the pressures on low- and high-skilled people, include not only economic but political considerations.

In countries that have closed the gaps at the secondary and tertiary levels but lack a large number of high-quality research centers or doctoral and postdoctoral graduate programs, investments in such programs make good sense. Several countries have innovative programs designed to repatriate and retain high-quality researchers, many of whom were trained at top universities abroad. In Mexico, for example, monthly grants are given to top researchers. The program helps repatriate Mexicans who completed their Ph.D.s abroad and who want to engage in scientific research activities in Mexico. By 2000 the program provided grants to about 7,500 registered researchers, 15 percent of whom had become involved through the repatriation program.

Policymakers also need to examine the pricing and financing of higher education, as well as taxation. In many countries, free or low-cost higher education combined with high marginal tax rates encourage high demand for higher education but also emigration.

Women, Technology, and Education

Gender inequality in access to all levels of schooling persists in most regions of the developing world, with the exception of Latin America. Gender differences in tertiary education enrollments are particularly pronounced in the Arab world, in some countries in Sub-Saharan Africa, and in South Asia. Even in countries where gender parity in education has been achieved, girls are often channeled into disciplines that lead to low-paying jobs. In Africa, Asia, and Latin America and the Caribbean, women's enrollment in engineering is low, ranging from less than 2 percent in Kenya to 27 percent in Colombia. In medical and health-related courses, female enrollment rates range from 25 percent in Kenya to 68 percent in Nicaragua (World Bank 2002d, 2002h). Throughout the world female participation in on-the-job training is significantly lower than male participation, in part because women often work in the informal sector or have lower educational attainment (OECD and Statistics Canada 2002).

The low level of education attainment by females has negative consequences for society as a whole, especially given the importance of mothers' education for student achievement. Results of the Programme for International Student Assessment (PISA) show that in reading, math, and science literacy, students whose mothers had received higher education performed considerably better than those whose mothers had received only primary or secondary education (OECD 2001e).

The implications of gender disparity in education are enormous given the importance of education in the knowledge economy. Much more effort needs to go toward achieving gender equity at the basic education level. While primary education is a foundation for further learning, however, it is clearly not enough. Countries must increase female participation at the upper secondary level. Ensuring equal access to higher levels of education and employment training, especially in science and engineering, is essential if a country is to be able to compete in the knowledge economy. Countries will not achieve education for all if gender inequality persists.

To expand the pool of women who pursue careers in science and technology, policymakers need to ensure that careers and role models are not stereotyped as gender specific. They need to develop measures to interest girls in science and math before they reach the tertiary level. Governments could, for example, train more female teachers in science and math, who could serve as role models for girls.

But targeting individuals is not enough. New institutional and organizational arrangements that ensure female students' access to higher levels of education must be created, women must be hired as faculty members, and female researchers must participate in research and development activities. At the same time, governments need to overhaul their own staffing policies and practices to interest more female science and engineering majors in public sector careers. More could be done to increase public awareness on gender equality by, for example, publishing statistics on gender inequality in job opportunities and wages. Increasing female participation in on-the-job training might require reform of labor regulations that allow employers to reduce women's access to jobs that provide such training (by hiring them only on a temporary basis, for example, or limiting promotion out of fear that women will have children and leave the labor force).

Employer Demands and Private Education Sector Responses

In the rapidly changing knowledge economy workers must constantly acquire new skills. In this environment, firms can no longer rely solely on new graduates or new labor market entrants as the primary source of new skills and knowledge. Instead, they need workers who are willing and able to update their skills throughout their lifetimes. To support the new demands, the private sector is playing a growing role in education and training throughout the world.

Employer Demands and Employee Training

In traditional industries most jobs require employees to learn how to perform routine functions, which, for the most part, remain constant over time (Nelson and Phelps 1966). Most learning takes place when a worker starts a new job—through formal and informal apprenticeship programs and informal on-the-job training, for example. During this initial training either the worker accepts lower wages while investing time in training (in which case the worker bears the costs) or the employer absorbs the costs in the form of forgone production by the trainee.

Learning also occurs in household production and community activities. This informal investment of time over the life cycle is a large and important part of the total investment in lifelong learning, but it is usually unobserved and undocumented.

The current rate of technological change has raised the skill requirements of most jobs and placed a premium on flexibility. Most workers require supplementary skills to remain competitive in their current jobs. Policies need to reflect this change, by creating incentives to keep people learning throughout their working lives (OECD 2001a).

In Colombia, Indonesia, Malaysia, Mexico, and Taiwan (China) training has a positive and statistically significant impact on firm-level productivity (Tan and Batra 1995). But not all workers have the same access to training. Employers do not train unskilled workers to the same extent as more highly educated workers. Tan and Batra (1995) found that larger firms, especially multiplant firms, are more likely to provide formal training for skilled workers. Enterprise training, especially in-house training, is most common at high-tech firms, firms relying on advanced technologies, firms with semi- or fully automatic production lines, and export-oriented firms. For workers in small or microenterprises, particularly firms that are not exposed to international markets and in which workers have low educational attainment, the gap between those who have access to skill upgrading—and hence higher productivity and higher wages—and those who do not will grow. With few exceptions government policies to encourage training in small and medium-size enterprises, through training levies or even grants, have not been very successful (Ziderman 2001). Providing such training represents a major challenge for all countries, especially those in which large proportions of the labor force work in the informal sector.

The provision of education and training is now a global market. The global market for education is estimated at more than $2 trillion a year (Moe, Bailey, and Lau 1999). In the late 1990s more than 1.5 million people pursued higher education outside their home countries, in a market worth almost $30 billion (WTO 1998). While one-third of the global market is in the United States, a sizable 15 percent is in developing countries and transition economies (Vawda and Patrinos forthcoming).

Corporations are spending more and more on training to become competitive in the global knowledge economy (box 1.4). International Data Corporation (www.idc.com) estimates that worldwide corporate training expenditures reached $28 billion by the end of 2002, up from $18 billion in 1997. In 1999 about one-third of the $100 billion for-profit education industry in the United States came from corporate and government training (Moe, Bailey, and Lau 1999; www.eduventures.com).

In another sign of the growing global market, the World Trade Organization (WTO) has begun negotiations over trade in services, including education. The General Agreement on Trade in Services (GATS) came into force in January 1995. It is the first and only set of multilateral rules covering international trade in services. Negotiated by governments themselves, it sets the framework within which firms and learners can operate. One of the most significant achievements of the Uruguay Round, the GATS offers for trade in services the same stability that arises from mutually agreed on rules, binding market access, and nondiscriminatory commitments that the General Agreement on Tariffs and Trade (GATT) has provided for trade in goods for more than five decades. However, education remains one of the sectors in which WTO members have been least inclined to make liberalization commitments (Larsen, Morris, and Martin 2001). By 2003, 53 countries had made commitments for at least one education subsector.

Growth of the Private Education and Training Sector

The private education and training sector is growing, not only in the United States and other industrial economies but also in low-income countries, including many in Africa. In the United States the number of two-year for-profit degree-granting institutions grew 78 percent and the number of four-year institutions grew 266 percent between 1990 and 2001 (Newman and Couturier 2002). In Brazil the number of tertiary education

Box 1.4. Transforming a Pulp and Paper Company into a High-Tech Leader: The Case of Nokia

Finland transformed its economy from one based on exports of natural resource–based products to one based on exports of high-tech products. As late as 1990, computer and telecommunications products accounted for less than 7 percent of Finnish exports; by 2000 the share had increased to nearly 30 percent. Finland made this transformation by steadily establishing an environment that enables innovation and the adaptation of technologies.

By the early 1900s Nokia, Ltd., was the largest pulp and paper mill in Finland. Three companies—Nokia, Finnish Rubber Works, and Finnish Cable Works—formed a conglomerate that drew heavily on imported technology. All three companies benefited from access to the large Russian market.

In 1967 the three companies merged, establishing four divisions: paper, cable, rubber, and electronics. For many years the electronics division was not profitable, but Nokia made sure that the division had access to the latest technology. By the early 1970s the electronics division grew with the expansion of the public radiotelephone system, originally developed by Finnish Cable Works.

In 1977 Nokia decided to transform itself from a producer of paper, tires, and cable to a global electronics giant. The company knew it lacked the necessary skills and experience to compete in the international market, however. Raising the level of human resources was essential for Nokia to be able to absorb and diffuse the skills and knowledge it obtained through acquisitions from, and strategic alliances with, technologically advanced foreign firms. It thus engaged in an aggressive human resource development program within the company that encouraged work abroad in foreign affiliates. At the same time Nokia's Chief Executive Officer, Kari Kairamo, was involved in modernizing the public education system, establishing broad international student-exchange programs, fostering continuous lifelong learning, and promoting close collaboration between industry and academia. By forming strategic alliances with foreign firms and strengthening human capital, Nokia prepared itself to compete in the global telecommunications market by the late 1980s.

Sources: Blomström and Kokko 2001; World Bank 2002d.

institutions grew more than 70 percent between 1995 and 2002, with most of the growth occurring in private colleges and universities, which accounted for 71 percent of higher education enrollment in 2002 (Souza 2002). In the late 1990s, 15–20 percent of all students in Côte d'Ivoire, Gambia, and Senegal attended private institutions. In Côte d'Ivoire, Gambia, Ghana, Senegal, and Zimbabwe, 11–14 percent of all primary education students attended private institutions. In Côte d'Ivoire enrollments in private institutions rose 20 percent at the primary level, 33 percent at the secondary, 140 percent at the technical/professional secondary, and almost 670 percent at the higher education level between 1991 and 1995. In Gambia private school enrollments increased 41 percent at the primary level, 123 percent at the junior secondary level, and 20 percent at the senior secondary level between 1993 and 1996. In Ghana enrollments in private primary schools increased 344 percent between 1986 and 1996 and accounted for 13 percent of all primary enrollments in 1997. In Senegal enrollments in private primary institutions increased 123 percent between 1987 and 1997, when they accounted for more than 12 percent of all primary enrollments (IFC 2001).

The private sector is growing rapidly in transition economies as well. Poland has 195 private higher education institutions, enrolling more than 377,000 students. Since the government gave permission for private universities to exist in the late 1990s, the Czech Republic has 26 private higher education institutions. Private business schools—unheard of in Eastern Europe 10 years ago—are also thriving: in 1998 there were 91 private business schools in Poland, 29 in the Czech Republic, 18 in Romania, and 4 in Bulgaria. Between 1995 and 1999, 500 new higher education institutions were established in China.

The growth of the private education sector signals an important change in the market for education. Clearly the demand for more and better education is increasing. The growth of the education industry in industrial countries has much to do with dissatisfaction with the traditional education and training system. It also reflects the fact that employers are looking for workers able to learn new skills while employed.

The global knowledge economy and the impact of technology on education are driving this change. Technology affects the delivery of education, giving an edge to providers able to offer flexible learning opportunities. In many middle-income countries, the private education sector is growing, a reflection of the need to expand schooling opportunities, relieve the fiscal burden, and promote innovation (Tooley 1999). Even in low-income countries private education is growing, in an attempt to keep up with technological developments and access global knowledge (Vawda and Patrinos forthcoming). Market forces are thus playing an increasing role in education around the world (Patrinos 2000).

2

Transforming Learning

In a time of drastic change, it is the learners who inherit the future. The learned find themselves equipped to live in a world that no longer exists.

Eric Hoffer, *Vanguard Management*, 1989

The challenges facing education and training systems in developing countries and transition economies are immense. They must raise the level of learners' achievement in the basic skills of language, math, and science. They must equip learners with new skills and competencies. And they must do all of this for more learners with different backgrounds, experiences, levels of motivation, and preferences. Achieving these goals requires a fundamental change in the way learning takes place and the relationship between learner and teacher.

Equipping Learners with the Skills and Competencies They Need to Succeed in a Knowledge Economy

Operating successfully in the knowledge economy requires mastery of a set of knowledge and competencies. Three categories of competencies are key (Rychen and Salganik 2001; OECD 2002a):

- *Acting autonomously*: Building and exercising a sense of self, making choices and acting in the context of a larger picture, being oriented toward the future, being aware of the environment, understanding how one fits in, exercising one's rights and responsibilities, determining and executing a life plan, and planning and carrying out personal projects.

- *Using tools interactively*: Using tools as instruments for an active dialogue; being aware of and responding to the potential of new tools; and being able to use language, text, symbols, information and knowledge, and technology interactively to accomplish goals.
- *Functioning in socially heterogeneous groups*: Being able to interact effectively with other people, including those from different backgrounds; recognizing the social embeddedness of individuals; creating social capital; and being able to relate well to others, cooperate, and manage and resolve conflict.

The concept of competency has several features. It is strongly related to context, combines interrelated abilities and values, is teachable (although it can be acquired outside the formal education system), and exists on a continuum. Possession of the key competencies contributes to a higher quality of life across all areas.

Performing in the global economy and functioning in a global society require mastery of technical, interpersonal, and methodological skills. Technical skills include literacy, foreign language, math, science, problem-solving, and analytical skills. Interpersonal skills include teamwork, leadership, and communication skills. Methodological skills include the ability to learn on one's own, to pursue lifelong learning, and to cope with risk and change.

These competencies are needed because of the rapid proliferation of scientific and practical knowledge, the shortening of the useful life of knowledge because of the continuous production of knowledge, and the growing influence of science and technology, which profoundly change the organization of jobs and lives. The consequences of these changes cannot be reliably foreseen (OECD 1996).

These skills also enable citizens to engage more actively in the knowledge economy. For example, advances in biotechnology raise many questions that society, not just scientists, need to answer. Being able to make decisions about these issues requires some ability to understand scientific concepts and knowledge. Zambia's decision in 2002 to return food aid because it contained genetically modified products is one dramatic example of a decision where scientific issues were central but perhaps not widely understood.

Measurement of interpersonal and methodological competencies is in its infancy, although some developments are underway. Social competence, for example, is assessed in the PISA, and new instruments for intercultural competence are emerging (Hammer and Bennett 1998; Göbel and Hesse forthcoming). Some private businesses use personality testing, and many companies and organizations are trying to measure interpersonal skills as part of performance evaluations. In no country, however, has a set of national (or even local) expectations of performance been established. In contrast, most countries have standards for technical skills, several of which have been tested in a comparable way in different countries.

Literacy

In low-income countries other than China and India, rates of illiteracy remain high. Overall, among people 15 and older, 29 percent of males and 46 percent of females cannot read or write. In contrast, illiteracy is negligible in high-income countries (World Bank 2000c).

Sobering as these figures are, they actually understate the ability of people in these countries to function in a knowledge economy, since they count as literate anyone who is able to read and write a simple statement. This level of literacy is insufficient for the knowledge economy, in which a secondary-level education is increasingly regarded as basic education. One of the main results of international studies has been the demonstration of the importance of basic skills. Higher-level competencies cannot be developed without fundamental and content-oriented knowledge.

The International Adult Literacy Survey (IALS) measures literacy performance at five levels, with level 3 the minimum required to function in the knowledge economy. The standard for literacy at this level includes the following (OECD and Statistics Canada 2002):

- *Prose literacy:* Learners should be able to locate information that requires low-level inferences or that meets specified conditions. They should be able to identify several pieces of information located in different sentences or paragraphs. They should be able to integrate or compare and contrast information across paragraphs or sections of text.
- *Document literacy:* Learners should be able to make literal or synonymous matches. They should be able to take conditional information into account or match up pieces of information that have multiple features. They should be able to integrate information from one or more displays of information and to work through a document to provide multiple responses.
- *Quantitative literacy:* Learners should be able to solve some multiplication and division problems. They should be able to identify two or more numbers from various places in a document. They should be able to determine the appropriate operation to use in an arithmetic problem.

Performance on the IALS varies considerably across countries (figure 2.1). Even in some high-income countries, sizable proportions of the adult population read below level 3. In all countries participating in

Figure 2.1. Literacy Levels in Selected Countries, 1994–98

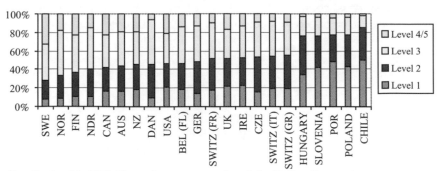

Note: Results of the IALS. Figures show percentage of population 16-65 reading at each prose literacy level. Countries ranked by percentage of population reading at levels 1 and 2.
Source: OECD and Statistics Canada 2000.

the IALS (mostly high-income or transition economies), adults with more education performed better than those with less education, and people with basic skills were less likely to become unemployed than those without (Murray, Kirsch, and Jenkins 1998; OECD 2001e). The effect is more pronounced at the lower levels of literacy, indicating that even a small increase in skill levels results in large social and economic effects. However, there is huge variation across countries in all types of outcomes for people with similar levels of education. In Finland, for example, only 10 percent of adults who completed upper secondary school could not read at level 3. In contrast, almost 59 percent of adults in the United States with the same level of education had not mastered level 3 literacy (OECD and Statistics Canada 1997).

The developing countries and transition economies that participated in the survey—Chile, the Czech Republic, Hungary, Poland, and Slovenia—performed poorly. Except in the Czech Republic, more than 25 percent of the population in each of these countries scored at level 1, and more than 75 percent fell below the level 3 threshold.

Mastering literacy early is important for giving young people access to learning. But many children in developing countries face a significant hurdle when they enter formal schooling because the language of instruction is not spoken at home. South Africa's poor performance on the Third International Mathematics and Science Survey (TIMSS) appears to be attributable in part to the high proportion of learners for whom English (the language of the test in South Africa) was a second language (Howie and others 2000). Children are more likely to enroll in school, learn more, and develop positive psychological attitudes in school and they are less likely to repeat grades or drop out of school when initial basic education is offered in their first language (or at least in a language they understand) (Klaus, Sedmihradsky, and Vancurova 2002).

Skills in an International Language

Policymakers in developing countries need to ensure that young people acquire a language with more than just local use, preferably one used internationally. Once children can read and write with confidence in one language, they are more easily able to learn another language (Klaus, Sedmihradsky, and Vancurova 2002), reinforcing the need for strong literacy skills.

More and more institutions of higher learning are offering courses in English. All private universities in Bangladesh and Pakistan, for example, except those providing Islamic education, offer instruction in English. People seeking access to international stores of knowledge through the Internet require, principally, English language skills.

Math and Science Skills and Knowledge

Competency in math and science is important for participation in the knowledge economy. Male student achievement in science has a statistically positive effect on economic growth, and that correlation is stronger than the correlation between growth and completion of upper secondary or higher education. Male achievement in math is also positively correlated with growth, although the effect is not as strong as for science. (Female achievement is not correlated with growth, probably because of discrimination in the labor market.) These effects appear to reflect broad-based scientific literacy, not just the effect of a small cohort of highly trained scientists working in research and development (Koda 2002).

The TIMSS is the largest comparative international study on the performance of students in math and science. It measures achievement at three different ages during primary and secondary education. Many transition economies, including the Czech Republic, Hungary, the Russian Federation, and the Slovak Republic, and some Asian countries, such as the Republic of Korea and Taiwan (China), performed well on this assessment, both relative to their per capita GDP and in absolute terms (figure 2.2).

Another international study, the PISA, measures learners' ability to apply their knowledge and skills in real-life situations (OECD 2001e). Transition economies ranked lower on the PISA, which measures the ability to apply knowledge, than they did on the TIMSS, which measures acquisition of knowledge (table 2.1).

Two facts are worth noting about these results. First, the two Asian countries that took part in both the PISA and TIMSS assessments—Japan

Figure 2.2. GNP per Capita and Student Achievement on the Third International Mathematics and Science Study in Selected Countries, 1999

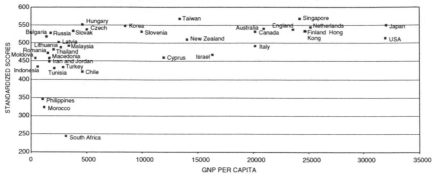

Source: Koda 2002.

and the Republic of Korea—performed well on both, belying the common notion that the Asian education systems are good at ingraining information but that Asian students lack the creativity to use and apply knowledge. Second, the relative performance of developing countries and transition economies was better on the TIMSS than the PISA.

Table 2.1. Performance of Selected Countries on TIMSS and PISA International Assessments in Science

Country	TIMSS		PISA	
	Average	Rank	Average	Rank
Hungary	552	3	496	15
Japan	550	4	550	2
Korea, Republic of	549	5	552	1
Czech Republic	539	8	511	11
England	538	9	532	4
Finland	535	10	538	3
Russian Federation	529	16	460	29
United States	515	18	499	14
New Zealand	510	19	528	6
Latvia	503	20	460	30
Poland[a]	n.a.	n.a.	483	21
OECD average	488	n.a.	500	n.a.

n.a. Not applicable.
a. Poland did not participate in the TIMSS.
Note: Differences in rank do not necessarily imply significant differences in performance.
Sources: Martin and others 2000; OECD 2001e.

The TIMSS, the PISA, and the IALS measure different things, but the results seem to lead to three broad conclusions (Koda 2002):

- A combination of factors, rather than any single feature, appears to explain countries' relative performance. This finding suggests that comprehensive reform initiatives are likely to have greater impact on achievement than more limited reforms.
- The socioeconomic status of schools had a greater effect on performance than did the socioeconomic background of students. This finding suggests that tracking students into schools with learners of similar backgrounds will reinforce inequalities. It also suggests a potential role for school choice to promote diversity of school populations.
- The organization of secondary schooling matters. According to Woessman (2001), 75 percent of cross-country variation in math and 60 percent of variation in science can be explained by institutional differences in educational systems. Factors that make a difference include central examinations, centralized control mechanisms in curricular and budgetary affairs, school autonomy in process and personnel decisions, incentives and discretion for individual teachers to select teaching methods, limited influence of teacher unions, teacher scrutiny of learners' educational performance, encouragement of parents to take an interest in teaching matters, an intermediate level of administration performing administrative tasks and educational funding, and competition from private educational institutions. While the hypothesis has not been rigorously tested, it appears that systems with well-defined vocational tracks in which large numbers of learners participate—as they do in the transition economies and in Germany—perform worse than other countries.

Participation in Civil Society

A 28-country study on citizenship and education (Torney-Purta and others 2001) examined knowledge of and participation in civil society (table 2.2). This measure is important because it is linked to good governance and the rule of law, which directly affect economic and social development.

Lower-income countries generally did not participate in these various international assessments, but it is likely that they would not have performed well. The range in performance at lower levels of per capita GDP, however, suggests that even with their more meager resources developing countries can improve their performance—by adopting some of the pedagogical changes discussed below, for example.

Table 2.2. Knowledge of and Participation in Civil Society in Selected Countries, 1999

| Country | Civic knowledge | Civic engagement | | Civic attitudes | | |
	Total	Conventional citizenship	Expected participation in political activities	Trust in government institutions	Positive attitudes about immigrants	Support for women's political rights
Australia	M	–	–	+	M	+
Belgium[a]	–	–	–	M	M	M
Chile	–	+	+	M	+	–
Czech Rep.	+	–	–	+	+	+
England	M	–	–	M	–	+
Estonia	–	–	M	–	–	–
Finland	+	–	–	M	M	+
Greece	+	+	M	+	+	M
Lithuania	–	+	–	–	–	–
Poland	+	+	+	M	+	M
Russian Fed.	M	–	M	–	M	–
Slovak Rep.	+	+	–	+	–	–
United States	+	+	+	+	+	+

Note: – indicates performance significantly below the international mean; + indicates performance significantly above the international mean; M indicates performance not significantly different from the international mean.
a. French-speaking Belgium only.
Source: Torney-Purta and others 2001.

Changing the Way People Learn

Traditional educational systems, in which the teacher is the sole source of knowledge, are ill suited to equip people to work and live in a knowledge economy. Some of the competencies such a society demands—teamwork, problem solving, motivation for lifelong learning—cannot be acquired in a learning setting in which teachers dictate facts to learners who seek to learn them only in order to be able to repeat them.

A lifelong learning system must reach larger segments of the population, including people with diverse learning needs. It must be competency driven rather than age related. Within traditional institutional settings, new curricula and new teaching methods are needed. At the same time, efforts need to be made to reach learners who cannot enroll in programs at traditional institutions.

Providing people with the tools they need to function in the knowledge economy requires adoption of a new pedagogical model. This model differs from the traditional model in many ways (table 2.3). Teachers and trainers serve as facilitators rather than transmitters of knowledge, and

Table 2.3. Characteristics of Traditional and Lifelong Learning Models

Traditional learning	Lifelong learning
• The teacher is the source of knowledge.	• Educators are guides to sources of knowledge.
• Learners receive knowledge from the teacher.	• People learn by doing.
• Learners work by themselves.	• People learn in groups and from each other.
• Tests are given to prevent progress until students have completely mastered a set of skills and to ration access to further learning.	• Assessment is used to guide learning strategies and identify pathways for future learning.
• All learners do the same thing.	• Educators develop individualized learning plans.
• Teachers receive initial training plus ad hoc in-service training.	• Educators are lifelong learners. Initial training and ongoing professional development are linked.
• "Good" learners are identified and permitted to continue their education.	• People have access to learning opportunities over a lifetime.

more emphasis is placed on learning by doing, working on teams, and thinking creatively (box 2.1).

The lifelong learning model enables learners to acquire more of the new skills demanded by the knowledge economy as well as more traditional academic skills. In Guatemala, for example, learners taught through active learning—that is, learning that takes place in collaboration with other learners and teachers, in which learners seek out information for themselves—improved their reading scores more and engaged more in democratic behaviors than learners not in the program (de Baessa, Chesterfield, and Ramos 2002) (box 2.2). In the United Kingdom learners taught thinking skills in science were able to improve their performance in other subjects, and the effects increased over time (Adey and Shayer 1994).

How People Learn

Cognitive research on learning suggests that "how people learn is more important than what people learn in the achievement of successful learning" (OECD 2001h, p. 20). This work has shown that when the right tools and strategies are adopted and learners are motivated, most children can

---

Box 2.1. Encouraging Creativity in Singapore

Singapore's leaders have been rethinking that country's economic and education policies to ensure that they meet the challenges of a knowledge-based economy. In 1997 they launched the Thinking Schools, Learning Nation (TSLN) framework. One of the four pillars of the framework is the emphasis on critical and creative thinking in schools. Specific changes made to encourage creativity include the teaching of thinking skills and the introduction of interdisciplinary and project work.

Singapore has adopted a framework that relies on the belief that creativity can be taught. This assumption underlies its Dimensions of Learning program, in which learners are taught eight core skills: focusing, information-gathering, remembering, organizing, analyzing, generating, integrating, and evaluating. This approach is probably appropriate for a country that excels in math and science rather than the arts.

Sources: Australia, DEET 2002; Brown and Lauder 2000; Sharpe and Gopinathan 2001.

---

learn almost anything (Bransford, Brown, and Cocking 2000). Remedial learners placed in an accelerated pre-algebra program reportedly learned more than their peers in remedial math programs (Peterson 1989). Moreover, the learners placed in remedial programs lost ground compared with "regular" learners, whereas some of the remedial learners in the

---

Box 2.2. What Does a Learner-Centered Classroom Look Like?

Guatemala's Nueva Escuela Unitaria (NEU) program tackles some of the country's poorest and most isolated rural schools. The classrooms in the program reflect the program's learning-centered model:

". . . one seldom observes any large-group, teacher-dominated instruction. Rather groups of two to six students at a particular grade level can be seen working at a table, a learning corner, the library, or outside working in their self-teaching workbooks. The large chalkboard has been removed from most NEU classrooms, and while these classrooms generally have more instructional materials than a traditional, poor rural school, it is the way materials are used by students rather than their quantity that is exceptional in these classrooms. The library, always under student management, is meant to be used during the school day and books borrowed overnight rather than kept under lock and key. . . . [Evaluations] indicate a very low level of student discipline problems and an extremely high interest level by students 'doing their work.'"

Source: Craig, Kraft, and du Plessis 1998, p. 89.

accelerated program were able to shed their remedial designation. The difference in outcomes appears to be related to the methods used in the two classes. In traditional remedial programs, learners are drilled on low-level tasks. In contrast, in accelerated programs learners are expected to be able to tackle higher-level tasks and understand the conceptual under-pinnings of the subject.

The importance of early experiences in the development of the brain and subsequent behavior is well known (Fuchs and Reklis 1994; Mustard 2002; Osborn and Milbank 1987). The development of certain language learning processes (for example, the learning of grammar) depends on a particularly sensitive stage of development that is expected to occur during a specific time window. Other language learning processes, however, such as mastery of semantics, do not take place only during a particular period; these processes are not constrained by time or age (Greenough 2000). Changes in the brain previously thought to be associated with adolescence have now been shown to continue into one's twenties (OECD 2001g).

The material to which learners are exposed and the way they are taught are also significant. Sixth grade students who were introduced to certain concepts using learner-centered methods were better able to solve conceptual physics problems than 11th and 12th graders in the same school who were taught physics using traditional methods (White and Frederickson 1997).

Some observers distinguish adult from child learning because adult learning is said to be self-directed (Houle 1961). In fact, learning at any age can be characterized by how self-directed it is. Adults who know little or nothing about a topic benefit from teacher-directed instruction until they have enough knowledge to begin directing their own learning (Merriam 1993). Content and pedagogy are thus inextricably linked.

Characteristics of Effective Learning Environments

Effective learning environments are environments based on the ways people learn. They differ from traditional learning settings in that they are learner centered, knowledge rich, assessment driven, and community connected (Desforges 2001; Bransford, Brown, and Cocking 2000).

Learner Centered

A learner-centered environment recognizes that learners acquire new knowledge and skills best if the knowledge and skills are connected to what they already know. Teachers need to know what learners already know and understand before introducing new material. Learner-centered learning produces different outcomes from rote learning and direct teaching, where teachers are the source of knowledge and their job is to provide knowledge to learners, who receive it passively, if at all. Rote learning enables learners to retrieve and write down information in a narrow range of settings, such as examinations, but it does not teach students to connect what they learn or integrate it with what they already know. Learner-centered learning allows new knowledge to become available for use in new situations—that is, it allows knowledge transfer to take place.

Knowledge Rich

Learners' ability to transfer what they learn to new contexts requires a grasp of themes and overarching concepts in addition to factual knowledge. Knowledge-rich learning thus favors teaching fewer subject areas in depth rather than covering more subjects in less depth (Martin and others 2000; Mullis and others 2000). This kind of learning provides learners with a variety of strategies and tools for retrieving and applying or transferring knowledge to new situations. It also equips them, for example, to assess the tradeoffs between accuracy and speed of different strategies.

One of the best ways to develop these strategies is for learners to try to solve real or simulated problems using the knowledge and concepts being taught (Schank 2001). The tradition of learning by doing is long and rich, particularly in apprenticeships and many vocational courses. It has not been central to general education, however, for pedagogical reasons (the prevalence of teacher-directed approaches and the emphasis on "brain work" rather than "manual work") or practical concerns (logistics and the need to cover a broad curriculum) (Bransford, Brown, and Cocking 2000). It is important, however, because people learn some things implicitly. People often learn about the environment without intending to do so, in such a way that the resulting knowledge is difficult to express (OECD 2001g). In learning by doing, learners grasp many details that are difficult or tedious to make explicit.

Assessment Driven

Assessment-driven learning is based on defining clear standards, identifying the point from which learners start, determining the progress they are making toward meeting standards, and recognizing whether they have reached them. Assessment-driven learning helps the educational system define the instructional action plan, which needs to reflect the different places from which learners start. Giving learners—even very young learners—a role in the process of tracking their learning achievements and, especially, engaging them in discussion of the outcomes of these assessments are powerful motivators and tools for improved and independent learning.

Ongoing assessment and feedback is underused in traditional teaching settings. It has the greatest effects in terms of promoting the development of higher-order thinking skills and conceptual understanding (Bransford, Brown, and Cocking 2000).

Community Connected

The circumstances in which learning takes place have an important effect on the way people learn and the likelihood of a successful outcome (Merriam 2001). The setting—the classroom, the school, the institution, the virtual space—must be conducive to learning and to increasing learners' motivation. The teacher must create an atmosphere of trust, since understanding and rectifying mistakes are important elements in the process through which understanding develops.

It is important that learners be able to learn from one another. Giving learners the opportunity to work on joint projects is important for both children and adults (Merriam 2001). Implicit learning is linked to participation in successful social interaction (OECD 2001g).

It is also important to link activities inside the classroom with what is happening outside the classroom. Working on real-life problems or issues that are relevant to participants increases interest and motivation and promotes knowledge transfer (Cibulka and others 2000; Oxenham and others 2002). Moreover, important sources of information and knowledge exist outside the classroom that learners need to understand and access. These links can take many forms. Apprenticeships that involve alternating periods of institution-based learning of knowledge foundations coupled with the acquisition of work-related skills, competencies, and practices in the workplace are examples of this kind of linkage.

Aligning the Four Characteristics of Effective Learning Environments

The four characteristics of effective learning environments need to be aligned. Encouraging the development of thinking skills in learners will flounder, for example, if assessment is done through multiple choice tests that assess factual recall. In Jamaica the Reform of Secondary Education (ROSE) program developed new textbooks and trained all teachers in the use of a child-centered pedagogy. But teachers and parents expressed concern about whether the new approach would improve student performance on the end of schooling Caribbean Examinations Council examinations, which are traditional examinations of academic content (World Bank 2001g).

Implications for Teachers and Teacher Training

In the old model of learning, teachers told learners what they needed to know. In the new learning environment, teachers and trainers work as facilitators, enabling learners to access knowledge and develop their conceptual understanding. Creating this new environment requires a change of culture, especially where teachers' status in the classroom and society arises from being perceived as an authority figure.

Traditionally, teachers were learners only during pre- and episodic in-service training. Today they need to be lifelong learners. Teachers' and trainers' conceptions of teaching and learning, and their initial knowledge and understanding of their curriculum area, are the starting points. If they are ignored, it is likely that new pedagogical practices will not be accepted or will be misunderstood and therefore misused or misapplied (Desforges 2000).

Teachers need in-depth knowledge of their subject area, including knowledge of relevant facts, an understanding of the major concepts, and the connections between them. Evidence from the United States suggests that student achievement is higher when teachers have a minor or major university degree in the field they teach (Wenglinsky 2000; Kaplan and Owings 2001). In developing countries, too, teacher quality (as measured by education, knowledge, experience, and proficiency) and basic inputs (such as textbooks and instructional time and the demands made on learners) have been linked to higher student achievement (Scheerens 1999).

Teachers also need to know how to teach their discipline (Van Driel, Veal, and Janssen 2001). The way learners come to understand—or mis-understand—a subject varies from subject area to subject area. Teaching methods that work well in math may not work well in art or geography (Blansford, Brown, and Cocking 2000).

Like other learners, teachers need to learn by doing. They must practice and use the techniques they are expected to use in the classroom (Navarro and Verdisco 2000), then reflect on the experience, come up with more ideas, and try something new. Training must be relevant to the conditions teachers are likely to find in the classroom, which may include disadvantaged or diverse learners. Teachers with a good knowledge of their subject and who "had learned to work with learners who came from different cultures or had special needs [had students who] tested more than one full grade level above their peers" (Kaplan and Owings 2001, p. 4). An effective way to ensure a strong connection between training and what happens in the classroom is to train teachers in the classroom or at least at the school.

The environment in which teachers operate affects their ability to apply what they learn from training. Structural constraints can prevent teachers from applying what they learn, causing them to revert to their old ways of teaching. For this reason cascade models of teaching training—in which a small group of teachers is trained who then train a larger group of teachers, who then teach yet other groups of teachers—are unlikely to be effective (table 2.4). Enough teachers need to be trained at a given school or institution to build a group supporting each others' struggles to apply new ideas.

Professional development needs to be more closely aligned with plans for school or institutional improvement. A learning organization can improve itself by learning from its mistakes and adjusting its structures and the way it works in response to new knowledge. But doing so

Table 2.4. Effective and Less Effective Teacher Education Strategies in Developing Countries

More effective strategies	*Less effective strategies*
• Most training takes place in schools, where trainees observe, assist, and teach. Training is done in both formal and nonformal settings.	• Training is done primarily at universities, normal schools, or the ministry of education.
• Training occurs throughout the teacher's career.	• Training is a one-time preservice phenomenon.
• Training emphasizes actual classroom teaching behaviors.	• Training emphasizes receiving certificates and diplomas.
• Groups or cohorts of teachers are trained together.	• Teachers are trained individually.
• Reform of teacher education is an integral part of curriculum and other reforms.	• Reform of teacher education is separate from other attempts to reform the system.
• The inspection system supports good teaching practice.	• Teachers are seldom supervised; when they are it is generally for punitive reasons.
• Training begins with teachers identifying needs and demands.	• Training begins with theoretical considerations, possibly connected to teacher needs and demands.
• Self-study and self-learning are critical.	• Only knowledge mediated by the ministry or universities is acceptable.

Source: Adapted from Craig, Kraft, and du Plessis 1998.

requires leadership that fosters collaboration on the common goal of the organization. Effective leadership must be supportive and shared, it must reflect shared values and vision, promote collaborative learning within the organization and incentives to use that learning to improve performance, create supportive conditions, and provide opportunities for peer review and feedback (Huffman and Hipp 2001).

This process of continuous refinement and adjustment contrasts with national reforms and other top-down changes (Venezky and Davis 2002). A professional community within a school promotes learning, provides technical support for innovation, and sustains teachers through a support system. This professional community can be extended beyond a single school. In the Microcentros Program in Chile, for example, teachers from different schools, supervised by provincial representatives, decide when to meet and which topics to focus training seminars on (Navarro and Verdisco 2000; see also Delannoy 2000). The Primary Teacher Mentoring Program in Balochistan, Pakistan, works in a similar way (Craig, Kraft, and du Plessis 1998).

Bringing about this change in the way teachers and trainers behave is difficult even in OECD countries (OECD 1998b), partly because teachers' motivation and needs vary depending on where they are in their careers (Cibulka and others 2000). Effecting change is even more difficult in developing countries. Spending on nonwage recurrent items, such as chalk, textbooks, science equipment, and teachers' professional development, is usually very low. Lack of accountability for teacher (and school) performance is the norm, especially where teacher unions are politically powerful. Deeply rooted cultural expectations about the role and status of teachers may also hinder change.

Using Technology to Transform Learning

ICT has the potential to improve the quality of learning, expand access to learning opportunities, and increase the efficiency of administrative processes (World Bank 2002c). These technologies can support changes in pedagogy and teacher training, deepening and extending planned changes. Before ICT can help improve learning outcomes, however, institutions must be reorganized and teachers must change the way they approach learning (Venezky and Davis 2002).

ICT changes the role of the teacher. In Chile and Costa Rica it has helped create a more egalitarian relationship between teacher and learner, with learners making more decisions about their work, speaking their minds more freely, and receiving consultations rather than lectures from their teachers (Alvarez and others 1998). The teacher's role is no longer to provide content but rather to work with learners to explore new territory.

In some areas, international content can be adapted and aligned with national and local curricula. The availability of on-line curricular material also suggests that developing countries may be able to reallocate funding for curricular development, devoting more funding to course development of subjects not available through ICT (such as local history, culture, and agriculture).

Only a few institutions in the world have used ICT to establish all of the elements of an effective learning environment. Venezky and Davis (2002) identified 94 exemplary schools in OECD countries. In these schools the initial struggles to learn the technology (survival stage) had been overcome: classrooms were becoming more learner centered, and technology had become infused in learning activities (impact stage) (see Mandinach and Cline 1994 for the stages of reform). Very few of the 94 exemplary schools had reached the innovation stage, in which curriculum and learning activities are restructured in ways that go beyond mandated procedures and content (box 2.3).

Computers

ICT can facilitate the move from learning-by-telling to learning-by-doing (Schank 2001). In science laboratories, simulation software can be used to reduce the time between collecting and graphing data, enabling learners

---

Box 2.3. Using Technology to Create an Effective Learning Environment in Australia

One of the best examples of the transformative use of technology in education, according to the OECD, is in the State of Victoria, Australia, where the Department of Education has developed many tools and services that are highly valued by schools. These include SOFWeb, the most popular educational web site in Australia (35,000 documents), used by two out of every three teachers; Schools Television, broadcast by digital satellite; and Curriculum@work, an on-line and CD-ROM one-stop shop for curriculum resources.

The State of Victoria has promoted innovation in teaching and learning practices through its Navigator Schools program, launched in 1995. These pilot schools have focused on creativity and cross-disciplinary learning, the integration of computers into the curriculum, and the role of the teacher as learner. Learners in these schools are engaged. They challenge teachers to provide a learning environment that leads to greater learning.

Sources: Toomey 2000; Australia, DEET 2002.

to spend more time discussing, analyzing, and interpreting the data. Pilots can begin learning to fly planes using simulators, reducing the risks and costs associated with training in airplanes.

Early computer-assisted instruction, from the 1980s and early 1990s, was often highly repetitive. While these applications improved performance relative to traditional instruction, they did so over a limited range and promoted only relatively low-level skills. In the United States these types of programs were actually tied to lower student performance on a national math test that demanded higher-level skills (Wenglinsky 1998).

Newer software, known as knowledge-based tutors, has been designed based on evidence from the cognitive sciences on how people learn. It is designed to change pedagogical practice and produce gains across more complex sets of skills. Studies of knowledge-based tutors suggest that they are much more effective than the earlier computer-assisted instruction (table 2.5). Learners in kindergarten through 12th grade in the United States who used Computer-Supported Intentional Learning Environment (CSILE, pronounced "Cecil") for science, history, and social studies performed better on standardized tests and came up with deeper explanations than learners in classes without this technology (Roschelle and others 2000). Although all learners using CSILE showed improvement, the effects were especially strong for learners categorized as low or middle achievers.

Computer simulations in laboratories have significantly improved learners' graph-interpretation skills, understanding of scientific concepts,

Table 2.5. Improvements in Performance Attributable to Computer-Assisted Instruction and Knowledge-Based Tutors

Instructional setting	Number of studies	Effect size	Increase in performance compared with traditional instruction (percent)
Computer-assisted instruction			
Elementary school	28	0.47	68
Secondary school	42	0.42	66
Higher education	101	0.26	60
Adult education	24	0.42	66
Military training	38	0.40	66
Overall	233	0.39	65
Knowledge-based tutors			
Higher education	1	0.97	83
Military training	1	1.02	84
Secondary school	1	1.00	84
Overall	3	1.00	84

Source: Capper 2000.

and motivation (Roschelle and others 2000). Simulation programs have also proved effective in middle schools. Middle school students who used ThinkerTools, a simulation program that lets them visualize velocity and acceleration, outperformed high school physics students in their ability to apply the basic principles of Newtonian mechanics to real-world situations. The software made science interesting and accessible to a wider range of learners than was possible using traditional approaches (White and Frederickson 1997).

Simulations are effective because they are based on learner-centered principles. They require learners to make explicit their underlying assumptions or implicit reasoning; let them visualize the consequences of their reasoning, reflect on those findings, and share them with others; provide pictorial representations and dynamic displays of physical phenomena that they can use as bridging analogies when incorporating and amending concepts; and provide graphical analysis to illustrate interrelationships of variables in an experiment (Muth and Guzman 2000).

Computers can also help assess learning and provide feedback. Some computer programs provide direct feedback to learners. Others provide feedback indirectly by enabling learners to instantly see the effect of changes to parameters in a model (Rochelle and others 2000) (box 2.4). E-mail can be used to provide rapid feedback to distance learners. To the extent that learners are able to study independently or in groups using computers, teachers have more time to work with individual learners.

The Internet

The Internet can vastly increase the knowledge resources available to an institution (box 2.5). But on-line materials based on the new pedagogy

---

Box 2.4. Using Intelligent Tutoring to Teach Air Force Technicians How to Troubleshoot Problems

The Sherlock Project uses computers to teach troubleshooting to U.S. Air Force technicians who work on complex machines involving thousands of parts. The project combines a computer simulation program and an expert coach, who offers advice when learners reach impasses. Reflection tools allow users to replay their performance and try possible improvements. Researchers evaluating the program concluded that 20–25 hours of Sherlock training was equivalent to about four years of on-the-job experience.

Source: Bransford, Brown, and Cocking 2000.

Box 2.5. Using the Internet to Educate Students and Teachers

Computer technologies are powerful means of connecting learning to real-world contexts. Through e-mail and the Internet, learners and teachers can communicate with each other and work on joint projects.

One project in which they are doing so is GLOBE, a collaborative on-line network linking secondary education students and teachers with scientists from more than 80 countries who study the environment. Learners collect local data on a particular issue. They then send the data to scientists investigating the phenomenon, who send the learners their feedback and post the data graphically on the GLOBE website (http://globe.gov) (Bransford, Brown, and Cocking 2000).

In the United States, the Public Broadcasting System's (PBS) TeacherLine, funded by a grant from the U.S. Department of Education, provides teachers with on-line professional development in math and technology integration. In collaboration with the International Society for Technology in Education (ISTE), the National Council of Teachers of Mathematics (NCTM), and leading educational producers, TeacherLine has developed facilitated modules and self-paced learning opportunities that teachers can access on-line anytime, anywhere. PBS member stations work with local education agencies to adapt TeacherLine to meet state and local standards and help deliver TeacherLine to teachers across the country. TeacherLine offers the Virtual Mathematics Academy, where teachers can explore NCTM's principles and standards on-line; modules (facilitated mini-courses offered through local PBS stations); and the Community Center, where teachers can access on-line chats, find links to resources, and collaborate with teaching professionals across the country (http://teacherline.pbs.org/teacherline/).

---

are still limited. A recent study of 500 educational sites found that only 28 percent used inquiry-based activities and just 5 percent included problem-solving or decision-making. In contrast, 42 percent of the sites featured rote learning and 52 percent involved mainly information retrieval (Mioduser and Nachmias 2002, cited in Venezky and Davis 2002). The number of useful sites providing instruction in languages other than English was even more limited.

Where the Internet is available to learners on a reliable and affordable basis, the teacher is no longer the sole authority in the classroom. The Internet changes the hierarchical relationship between teacher and learner, with learners able to explore new territory, guided by the teacher.

Once the Internet is available to learners in all countries, learners will no longer be at the mercy of poorly qualified teachers (Schank 2001). Students anywhere in the world, for example, will be able to download course content from the Massachusetts Institute of Technology (MIT), which the university is putting on-line free of charge.

Training Teachers to Use Technology

ICT can support changes in pedagogy and improvements in student learning. But merely purchasing and putting computers in the classroom will not improve outcomes. The effect of ICT on learning has at least as much to do with factors that are independent of the technology as it has to do with the technology itself (OECD 2002b). The introduction of ICT must be supported by, or supportive of, complementary reforms. A policy for ICT in education should foremost be an education policy.

ICT can help change the role of the teacher; it cannot be used to bypass the teacher. Teachers' attitudes are as important as their skills. If technology is introduced as part of a move toward a child-centered pedagogy, teachers must understand and want to promote the new model if it is to be successful (Murnane, Sharkey, and Levy 2002). Extensive teacher training in the new technology, especially in its use in the classroom, is needed (Hepp and others forthcoming) (box 2.6).

Development of other staff is also necessary. Principals and school managers play a key role in promoting a culture of innovation and learning that is supportive of the use of technology and the pedagogical changes it will bring about (Venezky and Davis 2002). The skills to maintain, repair,

---

Box 2.6. Encouraging Teachers in Chile to Learn How to Use Technology

As part of its reform and upgrading of basic education in rural areas, Chile created technology microcenters, which teachers can visit on a structured or informal basis to share ideas or obtain training on the use of ICT. The microcenters—and their monthly meetings—turned out to be ideal opportunities to incorporate joint design and reflection about the way to introduce technology in rural classrooms as part of the national ICT initiative. The facilitator who visited ICT school classrooms participated in the microcenters' monthly meetings, working with groups of teachers to design activities that they would carry out before the next school visit the following month.

Source: Hepp and others forthcoming.

and upgrade ICTs also need to be developed. As Hepp and others (2002, p. 38) note, "Unreliable technology is the best innovation killer."

Making Policy Choices about Technology

Policymakers have a range of choices about what technology to invest in, how to use it, and how to balance these investments against others. Books will continue to have an important place in all learning environments. Computers are important, although studies have not found a single ideal student-to-computer ratio (Venezky and Davis 2002). Having a computer for every learner is undesirable, however, because it reduces teamwork (Hepp and others forthcoming). In some cases technology can reduce costs—by reducing the need for libraries to pay for expensive subscriptions and postage for periodicals, for example (World Bank 2002c). E-learning programs used by companies principally as a cost-saving measure have failed to meet either their financial or learning objectives, however (Ashton n.d.).

Installing ICTs and training teachers to use them is expensive: hardware costs represent about 25 percent of total costs (teacher training, program development, maintenance, and so on) (World Bank 2001e). Around the world annual ICT costs range from less than $20 to more than $600 a learner (Cawthera 2001; Bakia 2000, cited in Grace and others 2001). In poor countries, where discretionary spending is limited, such expenditures represent an enormous burden.

In making decisions about computers, policymakers need to consider not just total costs but also the extent to which learners have access to and can use computers. In a primary school in Zimbabwe, for example, the relatively small number of learners with regular access to computers results in an annual cost of roughly $15 per learner (table 2.6). While low in international terms, this cost is high given overall spending on education in the country. If the school was able to increase the proportion of users in the school with regular access to computers to 80 percent, the annual cost would fall by roughly 70 percent, to about $4 a student.

Rural schools are often at a disadvantage in terms of ICT use, because the schools tend to be in poorer areas (reducing local contributions), have fewer students (increasing costs per learner), use multigrade teaching (increasing barriers to ICT use), and have less developed telecommunication infrastructures (potentially increasing investment and recurrent costs). Government action is needed to reduce these disparities. Some countries have already taken action. Chile is reaching rural schools through its Rural Education Program for Primary Schools (ENLACES) (Hepp and others forthcoming). Schools in South Africa have introduced computers and the Internet (box 2.7).

Table 2.6. Annual Computer Costs per User in Selected Countries

Setting	Cost per computer ($)	Learners per computer	Learners with regular use of computer (percent)	Annual cost per learner ($)	Annual cost per regular user if 80 percent of school community had access ($)
Barbados (1998)					
National program at primary level[a]	2,000	3:1	–	646	194
Turkey (1999)					
National program at primary level[a]	1,100	40:1	–	32	128
Egypt (1998)					
Secondary school	1,600	27:1	–	75	204
Israel (1998)					
School	1,850	11:1	–	210	–
Zimbabwe (2000)					
Primary school	1,125–842	29:1	100	15	4
High school (basic)	0	16:1	3	31	4
Telecenter (basic plus)[b]	250	18:1	–	365	23
South Africa (2000)					
Primary school	48	22.1	50	10	2
High school	210	11:1	7	96	15
Rural high school	1,000	4:1	12	193	8
College	916	2:1	100	110	28

– Not available.
a. Based on assumption that average school has 700 learners.
b. Centers were provided with refurbished computers.
Sources: Bakia 2000; Cawthera 2001.

World Bank Support for Educational Technology

The World Bank's growing support of educational technology reflects the importance it places on using technology, especially computers, to improve educational outcomes. In 1997 just 14 percent of the Bank's education lending went to technology. That figure rose to 40 percent in 2000 and 27 percent in 2001. Between 1997 and 2001 more than three-quarters of World Bank–financed education projects included distance education, education technology, ICT, or education management information system (EMIS) components. Preliminary estimates show that lending for these components ranged from $150 million to $500 million a year (Georgiades 2001).

Box 2.7. Affordable Models for ICTs in Rural Areas: Myeke High School, Kwazulu, South Africa

Myeke High School has neither grid electricity nor a landline telephone connection. But it does have 27 computers, including a computer lab with 20 computers. Since September 2000 it has also been connected to the Internet. Satellite technology transmits information to the school's PCs, while Global System for Mobile Communications (GSM) technology is used to send information from the PCs to the satellite. All of the computers are powered by a mixture of solar power and an electric generator fuelled by liquid propane gas.

Equipment, software, and a structure to house the equipment and furniture cost about $45,000. Annual costs are less than $50 per user, based on usage by about one-eighth of the school's students. If usage increased to 80 percent of students, the annual cost per student would fall to about $11. If 80 percent of the staff and community also used the computers, the annual cost per user would fall to just $8.

Source: Cawthera 2001.

Expanding Learning Opportunities

Access to learning opportunities is very unevenly distributed within and across countries (table 2.7). In low-income countries, secondary school enrollment rates are just 46 percent. Moreover, enrollment figures in developing countries tend to overstate access to education, because many of the students who are enrolled are overage.

For people already in the labor market, gaining access to learning opportunities is even more difficult. Even across and within OECD countries, rates of training vary considerably (table 2.8). In 1996, the year in which the IALS was conducted, less than half of adults participated in training in every country surveyed but Sweden. In Poland, a country

Table 2.7. Gross Enrollment Ratios in Low-, Middle-, and High-Income Countries, 1998

Income level	Primary education	Secondary education	Higher education
Low	97	46	8
Middle	119	69	12
High	103	106	62

Source: World Bank 2001i.

Table 2.8. Participation in Adult Continuing Education and Training, by Level of Initial Educational Attainment, 1996 (percent)

Country	Primary	Lower secondary	Upper secondary	Non-university higher education	University	Total participation
Sweden	27.0	46.7	52.8	66.6	70.4	52.5
New Zealand	6.8	37.8	52.0	60.4	71.5	47.5
United Kingdom	23.4	34.2	53.2	60.7	73.7	43.9
United States	10.3	21.0	30.7	54.9	64.2	39.7
Australia	8.8	27.0	50.6	39.4	60.8	38.8
Ireland	8.6	17.6	29.4	44.1	51.0	24.3
Poland	2.7	9.9	20.6	32.5	34.3	13.9

Source: OECD and Statistics Canada 1997.

undergoing profound changes, fewer than one in seven adults was enrolled in retraining. Similar patterns of access to training were found in Chile (the one non-OECD country included in the IALS), where few people reported participating in training (Araneda and Marín 2002).

People with the greatest access to continuing education and training are typically employed, have higher-level educational qualifications, are younger, and work in larger firms (O'Connell 1999), raising questions about equity. Surveys in Colombia, Indonesia, Malaysia, and Mexico (Tan and Batra 1995) and in Côte d'Ivoire, Ghana, Kenya, Zambia, and Zimbabwe (Nielsen and Rosholm 2002) reveal that larger firms conduct more training than smaller firms. Total training capacity in Kenya is estimated at less than 7 percent of the number of new entrants into the labor market, and most of this capacity is for pre-employment training (Haan 2002). Most of the research on labor market policies that offer vocational training for the unemployed indicates poor results (with important but narrow exceptions) and suggests that public resources would be better spent on job search and counseling services (Dar and Gill 1998). The jobs the unemployed most often find are much less likely to offer continuing learning opportunities. Thus even when they are effective, these programs represent only the first step in reducing the gap between those who do and those who do not have access to continuing learning opportunities.

People in countries in which a high proportion of employment is in the informal sector are especially disadvantaged. Since employers pay for most training, the unemployed or people who work in small companies— who are more often the poor and poorly educated and therefore most in need—are least likely to be able to access learning. Training markets for

---

Box 2.8. The Limited Supply of Training for Rural Development in Madagascar

Some 70 institutions currently provide education and training for rural development in Madagascar. Thirteen public and two private training institutions offer long certified training courses of study, for which entrance is generally selective. All of these institutions are in larger cities and charge tuition. In recent years these institutions have moved away from providing training solely for civil servants. Some 60 non-formal training centers, mostly managed outside the public sector, also operate in Madagascar. These centers generally provide one or more short (3- to 15-day) sessions on topics such as management, the technical aspects of production, the organization of farmers and producers, and family education. Tuition, where it is charged, is usually in kind or involves only symbolic payment. This network of institutions continues to exclude a significant proportion of rural adults and young adults from learning opportunities, because enrollment is designed for literate people. The programs, particularly those in the nonformal training centers, reinforce stereotypes and gender inequalities.

Source: Randriamiharisoa 2001.

---

the informal sector fail for both demand and supply reasons (Vishwanath and Narayan 2001) (box 2.8).

The expansion of learning opportunities will need to take place through at least two routes: by making traditional education and institutions more flexible and by using technology.

Making Traditional Education More Flexible

New types of institutions are emerging, particularly at the tertiary level, where nondegree institutions are growing in importance. These institutions, such as community colleges, usually offer courses in professional or vocational subjects. Often they also provide contracted customized education and training services to enterprises. The quasi-public Hungarian Regional Labor Development Centers, for example, earn about a third of their revenue from customized training. One center trains Ford Motor Company mechanics throughout Central and Eastern Europe. Training takes place in a laboratory furnished by Ford, which the Center uses for training when Ford is not using it.

Traditional public institutions are also changing to make face-to-face learning more accessible, although this trend is more evident in OECD

Figure 2.3. Proportion of Part-Time Learners in Higher Education in OECD Countries, 1997

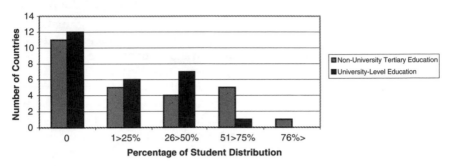

Source: OECD 1998a.

countries than in developing countries or transition economies. Part-time study at the tertiary level, in which learners take traditional on-campus classes in the evenings or over the summer, are well established in a few OECD countries, although even there the numbers remain low (figure 2.3). Private universities have typically been more flexible about offering part-time and night study. Part-time learners overwhelmingly are older and tend to be employed.

Many primary and secondary students also study in the late afternoon or evening. In Brazil about 60 percent of learners in upper secondary education attend night schools (World Bank and Inter-American Development Bank 2000). Double-shift primary and secondary schools are widespread in developing countries, where they reduce the opportunity cost of attending school by allowing students to work or perform family duties during part of the day. The quality of education in these schools appears to be as good as that in single-shift schools (Bray 2000). Schools usually operate two shifts in response to a lack of resources or facilities rather than to address learners' needs, however, and their lack of institutionalization makes them unattractive to parents (Linden 2001). For this reason, policymakers often seek to abolish them.

Using Technology to Reach More Learners

Distance education has a long and, under certain circumstances, successful history of providing education that is comparable to or better than that provided in traditional institutional settings in the same country. Although the evidence is more limited and ambiguous, these programs appear cost-effective as well.

Successful distance learning programs using traditional media (print, radio, and television) are operating at all levels of learning. Originally developed in Nicaragua in the 1970s, Interactive Radio Instruction (IRI) has been widely used at the primary level in many countries, including Bolivia, Kenya, South Africa, Thailand, and Venezuela. In Guinea and Lesotho it is being used on a national scale. IRI has been shown to be more effective than conventional teaching in math (World Bank 2001e; Perraton 2000).

In its original conception, radio instruction was designed to teach learners directly, using highly structured lessons with pauses for learners to respond or engage in learning activities. In recent years it has been used to supplement instruction and support rather than supplant teachers. In Guinea (World Bank 2001e) and South Africa (Perraton 2000), IRI has been designed to implement a child-centered pedagogy; in Kenya songs and games are used to involve learners in a more participatory way (World Bank 2001e).

The introduction of digital radio transmission should allow more countries to adopt IRI. Signal gaps that occur as a result of blockage by hills or buildings can be filled by installing very low power digital radio repeaters in these locations. Unlike conventional receivers, digital radio receivers can sort through several signal paths on the same frequency, a capability that will help conserve scarce radio spectrum.

Several digital initiatives are underway at both the national and global levels (Walker and Dhanarajan 2000). WorldSpace is a digital radio system targeting Asia, Africa, and South America through satellite transmission of digital programming. Community broadcasters can access national and international programs by rebroadcasting these programs, making them available to people who would otherwise not have access to them. Digital audio broadcasting also allows text- and graphic-based information to be displayed on a small screen on a digital radio as a supplement to the audio broadcast.

Television is the principal medium in the Telesecundaria program, which provides education to about 15 percent of lower secondary students in Mexico. The program uses high-quality broadcast materials, supplemented by workbooks, and local supervisors, who support learners. Evaluations have shown that it contributes significantly to learner outcomes (Perraton 2000).

Distance learning is also used for training. At Cisco Networking Academies in more than 145 countries, Cisco trains learners to become Cisco Certified Network Associates and Cisco Certified Network Professionals. The company uses the Internet to distribute up-to-date curricula to underserved populations, assess learner skills, monitor the quality of instruction, provide teachers with advice on technical and pedagogical issues, and enable teachers to keep track of learner progress and grades. The company's nearly 10,000 academies enroll more than 250,000 students, who learn how to design, build, and maintain computer networks (Murnane, Sharkey, and Levy 2002).

Teacher training at a distance is used principally for in-service training, either to train large numbers of recently hired but unqualified teachers (as it is in Botswana, Kenya, Malawi, Swaziland, and Uganda) or to upgrade teacher skills for the introduction of a new curriculum (as it is in China, India, and Pakistan). These models use correspondence and radio instruction, combined with some supervision of classroom practice (in China television has also been used). Several African countries are beginning to use ICTs in conventional teachers' colleges and teacher resource centers, usually in combination with other modalities (World Bank 2001e). In South Africa thousands of underqualified teachers now have access to ICTs. Pass rates on these courses have been very high; the salary increase following successful completion appears to be a powerful motivator. In the 1990s the distance learning program of the National Teachers Institute in Nigeria graduated more teachers than all other programs in the country combined (UNESCO 2001).

High completion and graduation rates make the use of distance education very cost-effective, especially when used in large-scale programs (box 2.9). The African Virtual University uses a mixture of taped and live lectures delivered by one-way video digital satellite broadcast with two-way audio and e-mail interaction between learners and instructors, supplemented by textbooks, course notes, and learner support in the classroom from facilitators.

Distance education at the tertiary level is well established, both in industrial and developing countries. Several open universities have more than 150,000 learners—China alone has almost 1.5 million open university students—and these students account for a significant percentage of higher education students in some countries (table 2.9).

Per learner costs at these institutions are lower than at traditional campuses, partly because distance learning programs rely heavily on printed materials and do not require buildings for students.

Distance education through any medium requires a basic infrastructure: a functioning postal system (important in all models); reliable sources of power (electricity or batteries); radio and television broadcast facilities; and receivers, satellites, or cables. The availability of different kinds of infrastructure, which varies significantly across countries (table 2.10), will necessarily influence decisions about the appropriate technology. It will also substantially increase costs if a new infrastructure needs to be put in place to handle a new kind of technology.

Distance education can be a cheaper way to provide education, but initial investments—especially the cost of developing materials and

---

Box 2.9. Using Distance Learning to Train Teachers in Mongolia, the Republic of Korea, and Sri Lanka

Traditionally, 85 percent of in-service funding for continuing professional development in Mongolia went toward travel, food, and lodging (UNESCO 2001). The use of distance education allowed the government to allocate a higher proportion of the budget to training, specifically to creating learning resources for teachers and funding more local workshops. The change increased teachers' access to learning opportunities. Instead of one week's professional development per primary teacher once every 10 years, teachers now regularly use distance learning to access radio, printed materials, and group meetings. These changes allowed Mongolia to train half of the country's teachers in six years.

In 1997 the Korean Ministry of Education and the Ministry of Information and Communication created a Cyber Teacher Training Center within the Korean Multi-Media Education Center. The Center developed 11 training courses and a software platform for managing the virtual teacher training. Along with an additional six courses developed in 1998, these virtual teacher training courses are now available through the edunet, an integrated educational service on the Web.

The Sri Lanka Institute for Distance Education (SLIDE) offers teacher development courses to untrained teachers using distance learning. Teachers study printed self-instructional materials, then receive supervised teaching and follow-up. They are supported through face-to-face sessions at regional centers and through study circles with other student-teachers. The teachers are supported for three to five years. Conventional courses take two years of full-time study in a teachers' college (Perraton 2000). About 5,000 teachers were studying with SLIDE in 1993. A 1990 evaluation found that the program was more cost-effective than the two conventional alternatives by a factor of 4.5–6 (Tatto, Nielsen, and Cummings 1991).

---

establishing the technological infrastructure (purchasing radios, televisions, and so forth)—can be high. Fixed costs have often been funded by external agencies (USAID was particularly active in the early years of interactive radio instruction). However, the proportion of fixed costs is typically higher for conventional education than for distance delivery (World Bank 2001e), highlighting the need to find a sustainable model of distance learning.

Table 2.9. Enrollment and Costs at Selected Open Universities, 1990s

Institution/country	Enrollment	Distance education enrollment as percentage of total tertiary learners	Distance education unit cost as percentage of campus unit cost	Learner fees as a percentage of distance education unit cost
China	1,422,900	24	25–40	–
Anadolu University, Turkey	470,072	26	–	–
South Korea National Open University	208,935	13	–	62
Indira Gandhi National Open University, India	182,000	11	40	26
Open University, Thailand	180,000	37	40	76
Universitas Terbuka, Indonesia	170,000	18	13	30
Open University, United Kingdom	154,200	8	39–47	43
University of the Air, Japan	68,000	4	13	–
Fédération Interuniversitaire de l'Enseignement à Distance, France	35,000	2	50	50
Open Learning Institute, Hong Kong (China)	20,000	21	–	86
Open University, Sri Lanka	16,400	32	–	30
Universiti Sains, Malaysia	5,500	3	73	–
National Centre for Distance Education, Ireland	3,500	5	43–66	70

– Not available.
Source: Saint 2000.

Table 2.10. Number of Radios, Televisions, and Personal Computers for Use in Educational Institutions in Selected Countries, 1997 (per 1,000 learners)

Region	Country	Number of radios[a]	Country	Number of televisions	Country	Number of personal computers
Africa	Angola	54	Ethiopia	5	Burkina Faso	<1
	Ghana	238	Uganda	26	Zimbabwe	9
	Malawi	256	Côte d'Ivoire	64	South Africa	42
Asia	China	195	Cambodia	124	Pakistan	4
	Malaysia	432	India	69	Singapore	399
Latin America and the Caribbean	Nicaragua	283	Ecuador	294	Guatemala	3
	Uruguay	610	Jamaica	323	Chile	54
Europe and Central Asia	Lithuania	404	Czech Rep.	469	Switzerland	348
North America	Canada	1,078	United States	847	United States	407

a. Data are for 1996.
Source: World Bank 2001e.

Many countries have struggled to meet the recurrent costs of distance learning. As a result, over time these programs tend to rely only on printed materials. Telecurso in Brazil, Telesecundaria in Mexico, and television universities in China are sustainable partly because they have many learners over whom to spread the costs of developing high-quality materials.

Successful distance learning programs allow learners to interact with a teacher, facilitator, or other learners. The secondary school study centers in Africa and the Chinese television universities are examples. The delivery of higher education to Chinese learners through television uses centrally prepared written materials combined with television programs beamed by satellite or recorded on video. What makes this model distinctive is that learning is a classroom activity. This classroom support provides answers to learners' questions plus assessment and feedback on performance—a key dimension of effective learning environments. Feedback is particularly important at the primary and secondary levels, where learners may not have the skills or motivation for self-directed learning (because of poor education or weaker support from communities and families, who may not themselves be literate).

The impact of ICTs on distance education at the primary and secondary levels has so far been marginal (Farrell 2001; Lizardi 2002). Many institutions of higher learning are offering on-line courses, however, sometimes in conjunction with other institutions. The National University of Singapore and MIT operate a joint master's program in engineering, in which learners from both campuses attend lectures conducted either at MIT or in Singapore. The program uses video conferencing through a high-speed broadband network (or VBNS) system in the United States, connecting to SINGAREN, Singapore's high-speed research network.

Virtual universities are an emerging phenomenon that offer maximum flexibility for learners. Many countries already have virtual universities, and countries as diverse as Jordan and Nigeria plan to develop them. New providers, such as private sector training, international providers, corporate universities, content brokers, and media, are also emerging to complement and challenge traditional institutions (World Bank 2002c).

ICTs are also changing the provision of learning opportunities in companies (table 2.11). In 2002 about one-quarter of U.S. corporate spending on education and training was delivered by technology, with e-learning making up about 20 percent of that share. In 1999, 92 percent of large corporations implemented Web-based training pilots (Urdan and Weggan 2000). Interestingly, soft skills training (that is, training in management, leadership, communications, team building, sales and marketing, human resources, and professional development) grew twice as rapidly as IT training.

Table 2.11. Demand and Supply Factors Driving E-Learning in Corporate Training

Demand	Supply
• Knowledge and training rapidly become obsolete.	• Internet access is becoming standard at work and at home.
• Training needs to be delivered on just-in-time basis.	• Advances in digital technologies enable creation of interactive, media-rich content.
• Businesses need cost-effective ways to meet learning needs of global workforce.	• Increasing bandwidth and better delivery platforms make e-learning more attractive.
• Skills gap and demographic changes require new learning models.	• Selection of high-quality e-learning products and services is growing.
• Flexible access to lifelong learning is needed.	• Emerging technology standards facilitate compatibility and usability of e-learning products.

Source: Urdan and Weggen 2000.

The Importance of Career Guidance and Counseling

If people are to take responsibility for managing their learning, they need information about themselves, the society in which they live, and the economy in which they function. Career information and guidance policies and services help provide the link between these sources of information and people's aptitudes and interests. They facilitate and promote lifelong learning. Developing countries, particularly middle-income countries, are increasingly recognizing the need to implement career development policies; industrial countries are strengthening existing policies and programs. The European Union and the OECD, along with their member countries, and more and more developing countries are refining policies and programs on career guidance. The OECD has begun a major study of career guidance policy (OECD 2000b). The World Bank is conducting a parallel study, scheduled to be completed in 2003.

Career development policies and services promote social equality and inclusion as well as access to educational and labor market opportunities. Guidance can perform a valuable role in raising the aspirations of the disadvantaged by making them aware of opportunities and supporting them in securing entry to such opportunities. Such services promote individual liberty and choice and emphasize the active individual.

Career guidance services enhance economic efficiency by making the labor market operate more effectively. Guidance can help ensure that the individual decisions through which the labor market operates are well informed. It can reduce market failures (drop-outs from education and training or mismatches between supply and demand). It can also support institutional reforms designed to improve the functioning of labor.

Conclusion

The challenge for developing countries—to provide a broader range of opportunities to acquire skills, knowledge, and competencies to more and more of their citizens—is immense. But the emergence of new providers, offering different services and in different ways, represents an opportunity for developing countries. It was not and is not possible to extend lifelong learning with the traditional model of secondary and higher education; the emerging modalities open the possibility that a learning system driven by the needs of learners can emerge. The hurdles to creating such a system are significant, however. Two more major issues, the role of governments in creating a lifelong learning system and how the system is to be financed, are addressed in the next two chapters.

3
Governing the Lifelong Learning System

I am growing old but still learning many things.

Solon (c. 650–555 B.C.)

As the first two chapters have shown, establishing a system of lifelong learning requires changes in the scope, content, and delivery of education and training (table 3.1). To create high-performance, lifelong learning systems, countries need to make significant changes to both the governance and financing of education and training.

Trends in Governance

Several broad governance trends are affecting all sectors, including education and training, across the world. The need to improve public sector management has become more pressing in both industrial and developing countries (Strange 1996; UNCSTD 2001), in part as a response to a more informed citizenry demanding transparency and efficiency in public sector management (World Bank Institute 2001b). The common trend in government reform has been the quest for smaller government through efficiency gains, achieved by drawing on private sector management principles of efficiency; new processes, such as performance management and reengineering service systems; greater focus on transparency of government operations; and a strong emphasis on outcomes and results (Kettle 1999). Governments are trying to harness the power of information and communication technologies to push ahead with these reforms. E-government is giving citizens greater and more rapid access to information about the policies and outcomes of government (see, for example, Heeks 2001). There is evidence that e-government, greater access to

Table 3.1. Scope, Content, and Delivery of Education and Training in Traditional and Lifelong Learning Models

Dimension	Traditional model	Lifelong learning model
Scope	• Formal schooling from primary to higher education	• Learning throughout the lifecycle—in schools, on the job, after retirement
Content	• Acquisition and repetition of knowledge • Curriculum driven	• Creation, acquisition, and application of knowledge • Diverse sources of knowledge • Empowerment of learners • Competency driven
Delivery	• Limited learning options and modalities • Formal institutions • Uniform centralized control • Supply driven	• Multitude of learning options, settings, and modalities • New pedagogical approaches • Technology-supported delivery • Pluralistic, flexible decentralized system • Learner driven

information, and improved public expenditure management systems have already produced efficiency gains—in the implementation of diagnostic Public Expenditure Tracking Surveys (PETS) in Ghana, Tanzania, and Uganda (Reinikka and Svensson 2002), for example, and the review of public school teachers' payroll systems in Argentina and Mexico (World Bank 1998e). A critical aspect of these reforms is the extent to which people in government view the information they have as a public resource, to be shared and subject to standards (UNESCO and COMNET-IT 2002).

Developing countries face a range of challenges to move forward with this agenda, in particular the need to increase transparency in the governance process. Transparency can be understood as openness about policy intentions, formulation, and implementation and the absence of corruption (World Bank 1997). The fight against corruption—including the fight against the loss of resources designated for education—has become a policy focus in developing countries (World Bank 2000b). NGOs active in education have monitored government performance by tracking education expenditure and outcomes and the extent to which earmarked resources go to specific programs or population groups. These trends provide the context for the dimensions of governance examined in this chapter.

In many OECD countries the role of government in the learning system has shifted from focusing principally on public financing and provision of education to creating a flexible policy and regulatory framework that encompasses a wider range of institutional actors and partners. In this context the main governance challenge is to promote efficient coordination mechanisms and to put increased emphasis on individual learners. This framework needs to be enabling, inclusive of disadvantaged learners, and responsive to learners' needs (table 3.2). Within this framework incentives assume a greater importance than rigid policy directives and control from government. The framework includes legislation and executive orders; arrangements for ensuring coordination across ministries and other institutions involved in education and training activities; and mechanisms for certifying the achievements of learners, monitoring institutional and system performance, and promoting learning pathways.

Coordinating Policy across Ministries

Critical in a lifelong learning perspective are coordination between line ministries in the central government as well as close linkages between general education and vocational education, and training on the one hand and education and work on the other. To promote coordination

Table 3.2. Traditional Role of Government and New Role in the Knowledge Economy

Policy issue	Current role	Role in the knowledge economy
Integration/coordination at national level	Adopts compartmentalized, sectoral approach	Coordinates multisectoral approach
Coordination across governance levels	One-way control and regulation	Two-way mutual support and partnerships
Government as an enabler	Controls and regulates	Creates choices, provides information and incentives, facilitates cooperation and provision
Linkage between education and the labor market/society	Supply is institution-driven	Demand is learner driven
Qualification assurance system	National standards, linked with curriculum and student assessment	Diverse system of recognition and quality control
Administration and management	Provides rules and regulation	Creates incentives, facilitates diverse providers

several OECD countries have combined central ministries. In 2001 the Korean government upgraded the Ministry of Education, renaming it the Ministry of Education and Human Resource Development (MOEHRD). Headed by a deputy prime minister, MOEHRD coordinates the policies of line ministries (for example, the Ministries of Labor, Science and Technology, Information and Communication, and Economy and Finance) that have implications for human resource development and lifelong learning. In similar moves, Germany created the Federal Ministry of Education and Research in 1998 and Japan created the Ministry of Education, Culture, Sports, Science and Technology in 2001. Other countries have developed knowledge and learning strategies that require coordination between education and training ministries and ministries that deal with such issues as early childhood development, science and technology, information and communication technology, industry, trade, and finance. Australia and the United Kingdom, which had combined education and employment ministries, have now separated them to ensure that Cabinet-level discussions focus equally on learning and economic issues.

Under the World Bank Lifelong Learning and Training project, Chile is horizontally and vertically changing the way it validates skills acquired on the job or in training institutions and revamping the coverage and quality of tertiary technical education. Vertically, the curriculum offered in grades 11 and 12 in all technical secondary schools is being aligned with that offered in tertiary institutions' technical and professional courses. The horizontal alignment attempts to link education quality and labor market demands by establishing local collaboration between the business sector and training institutions (World Bank 2002b). In addition, the national government has created a council, headed by the minister of finance and including the ministers of education and training, to oversee the project. Though these reforms are based on good practice elsewhere, it is too early to determine whether these structures as developed in Chile will be effective.

The Nordic countries have shown that coordination pays off in improving the transition rates of young people from initial education to working life. In these countries most graduates immediately find jobs, youth unemployment is low, and almost all young people are either in school or working. These countries have achieved these results by emphasizing both prevention and remediation (with a focus on rapid reintegration of school drop-outs); integrated education, labor market, and welfare policies (using subsidized employment to increase skill levels, not just provide young people with jobs); and delivery mechanisms that, critically, are managed at the local level and have responsibility for and ability to coordinate across several agencies (for example, education, employment, health, welfare, and police) at different levels of government (OECD 2000c). Such a system requires a clear framework for action, adequate resources, and, especially, administrative capacity to track individuals and work across ministries and levels of government.

Finland has used policy coordination to develop an effective lifelong learning system that starts with a vision of lifelong learning. Its lifelong learning strategy begins by offering all children access to preschool education. After completion of compulsory schooling, young people are encouraged to enter upper secondary general or vocational education and to complete their studies. Finland offers many non-university higher education programs, and it provides opportunities for adults to study for university degrees. It is also developing methods for recognizing nonformal and informal learning.

The strength of the Finnish economy and the opportunities that exist for lifelong learning owe much to the development of a comprehensive and inclusive education and training system and significant investment in human capital (box 3.1). As a result of that investment, Finland's students are among the best educated in Europe, placing first in reading, third in science, and fourth in math in the Programme for International Student Assessment (PISA) (OECD 2001e).

Box 3.1. Systemic Reform for Lifelong Learning in Finland

For decades Finnish education policy has focused on improving the overall level of education and ensuring equal access to lifelong learning for all groups in all regions of the country. School-age students are required to attend formal schooling. The system also provides opportunities to participate in and complete any level and form of education and training after school age.

Finland's national statement outlines its vision of lifelong learning. That vision includes:

- Providing one year of preschool education for all children before comprehensive school.
- Helping more young people apply for and complete upper secondary general or vocational education.
- Developing students' learning skills in all sectors of the education system.
- Increasing the provision of non-university higher education.
- Expanding opportunities for adults to study for a university degree.

(continued)

Box 3.1. (*Continued*)

- Expanding opportunities for adults to study for upper secondary and postsecondary vocational qualifications and to pursue other studies that improve their employability and capacity for further learning.
- Developing methods for recognizing nonformal and informal learning.

The government provides many incentives to encourage people to pursue education throughout their lives. Compulsory comprehensive schooling, upper secondary education, and vocational education are free. Students pursuing compulsory education through upper secondary schools receive free meals, and meals for higher education students are subsidized. Student housing is free for upper secondary and vocational education students. Financial aid is available for full-time post-compulsory studies.

Since 1992 Finland has also been developing alternatives to university studies. Its polytechnic schools offer shorter, more practical courses of study in technology and engineering that meet the needs of high-tech industry.

Except for university education, adults can participate in all levels of certificate- and noncertificate-oriented education. Adults can also complete primary or general upper secondary education and take part in the matriculation examination. Provision of basic education for adults (except for compulsory education) is not as strictly regulated as compulsory education. The 1999 Vocational Education Act caters to the needs of adults, providing, for example, the opportunity to pursue distance learning. Finnish universities do not offer special arrangements for adults, but adults account for one-fifth of students at the polytechnics. Various types of noncertificate-oriented courses are also available to help adults upgrade their skills, and financial support for adults is available. In 1998, 58 percent of Finns between the ages of 25 and 64 reported having participated in learning within the previous 12 months, the highest in the OECD.

Sources: Kartovaara 1996; OECD n.d., 2001c, 2001i, 2002c.

In some developing countries, such as Jordan and Mauritius, many ministries often oversee, manage, and finance training, and competition for scarce resources prevents collaboration, promotion of high-quality training, and a continuum of training opportunities. Elsewhere, as in Turkey, a single ministry is responsible for both vocational and general education, but there are several specific types of vocational schools. Since each type has its own hierarchy within the ministry and its own curriculum, management, and financing, the result is a fragmented and ineffective approach.

Vertical coordination, in the form of policy guidelines and budget/subsidy allocation from the center to the regions, will remain important as countries continue to decentralize their education policy decisions and implementation plans, which in turn will determine the quality and equity of education. Vertical coordination is particularly challenging in transition economies, which only recently moved from centralized command and control systems. Under those systems, at least in theory, coordination was simple, as subnational units were merely implementation agents of the central government (World Bank 2000a).

Forming Partnerships with the Private Sector and Civil Society

The state will have to play a more pluralistic role in providing, financing, and managing education. It will no longer be the (almost) sole provider and financier of education but will have to cooperate with the private sector (both for-profit and not-for-profit institutions) and civil society, using comparative advantages and synergies to reach common education goals more effectively and more efficiently (OECD 2001d).

The private sector can provide education in both traditional ways (owning and operating private schools and providing inputs, such as books, materials, and equipment) and novel ways (operating public schools under contract). Enterprises also provide training and are increasingly involved in developing occupational standards and curricula.

Policymakers need to create a level playing field between public and private providers. They can do so by, for example, ensuring that publicly funded student loan programs can be used at private institutions (as in the United States) or at institutions that offer distance programs, short-duration training, or other nontraditional courses; by ensuring that subsidies to publicly managed institutions do not crowd out private providers in the same fields; and by adopting accreditation procedures that guarantee quality and protect learners from fraudulent practice, while respecting the institutional diversity that private institutions bring.

Another way in which the private sector can participate in education is for nongovernmental organizations to operate public primary and secondary schools or take responsibility for parts of the curricula in public schools on behalf of the government. Examples include Fe y Alegría in Venezuela (and many other Latin American countries); the SABIS School Network in the Middle East, the United Kingdom, and the United States (box 3.2); and Cisco Systems, which has established "academies" in more

---

Box 3.2. Forming Creative Partnerships between the Public and Private Sectors to Run Schools

Established in Venezuela in 1955, Fe y Alegría (FyA) is a regional federation of national educational organizations, each of which provides a wide range of educational services in highly marginalized communities. Services focus primarily on delivery of formal primary education and technical training, ranging from farming to secretarial skills. FyA now serves schools in 14 countries, reaching more than 800,000 students. Governments provide some funding to FyA schools, to meet operating or set-up costs. In 1998 FyA was allowed to take over three failing public schools in two poor neighborhoods of Caracas, Venezuela. Under an agreement with the government, it leased the buildings for 50 years and operates the schools.

The SABIS School Network is a network of 22 public and private schools serving more than 18,000 students in the Middle East, the United Kingdom, and the United States. Each school is financially and administratively independent. All schools use the SABIS Educational System, which consists of an internationally oriented college-preparatory curriculum emphasizing English, math, science, and international languages.

Sources: O'Donoghue 1998; World Bank reports.

---

than 145 countries that offer computer networking qualifications recognized in the labor market. The Universitas 21 consortium brings together 17 major public and private universities from around the world with a publishing company to develop and deliver distance education courses internationally (www.universitas21.com). Heineken reached an agreement with unions in the Netherlands that included a guarantee that all current employees would continue to be employed by the company but that they would undergo training, individually or collectively, for their new functions. Redesign was worked out from the bottom up, with trade union representatives and work counselors working on design teams (European Industrial Relations Observatory Online 1999). Enterprises are often the most important providers and financiers of training for workers, even in the poorest countries (Johanson 2002).

Developments in education and training delivery mean that, increasingly, the capabilities needed to improve and transform the education and training system will reside in the private sector. Private media and publishing houses and technology-driven manufacturing companies already have the skills and knowledge to develop Web-based and multimedia courses and materials for distance learning.

Developing countries face significant challenges in attracting competent personnel to fill creative, technical, and managerial positions in the education sector, especially where the sector is dominated by public sector terms and conditions (Grace and others 2001). Teachers trained to use new technologies, and math and science teachers, can often find more remunerative jobs outside the education sector. Part of the solution to attracting them to teaching lies in increasing the number of technically competent people, thereby reducing the premium for these skills. The need to do so underscores the point that solutions to problems in the education and training sectors often require cross-sectoral approaches. Another part of the solution may be more flexible pay scales and conditions of employment.

Framework for Quality Assurance

New quality assurance mechanisms which certify learners and accredit institutions are needed to promote lifelong learning. This is because existing arrangements do not capture new and important skills and competencies, nor do they value informal and nonformal learning.

Certifying Learners' Competencies

Learning needs to become more flexible and diverse to allow alternative delivery mechanisms, such as distance education and e-learning, open entry and exit, flexible enrollment, modular courses, and training that is available as and when needed. As this happens, learners' acquisition of skills and more and more learning will take place outside of formal educational institutions. In addition, a new and diverse set of competencies and skills, described in chapter 2, will be acquired in various nonformal out-of-school learning activities, as well through formal channels.

These changes call for a more flexible system of recognizing learning. Such a system should promote alternative pathways for learners within and between different levels of institutions. It should provide linkages between different types of qualifications, vocational and academic. It should articulate training standards and qualifications that help link formal and informal education and training and integrate learning, licensing and qualifications, and labor market needs (box 3.3). It should also enable learners to have their achievements recognized across countries.

A learning certification system needs to recognize nonformal learning to provide incentives for people who have not completed a level of schooling or who are engaged in nonformal learning. This is particularly important in developing counties, where access to formal education and training institutions is limited.

Box 3.3. Building a Lifelong Learning System in Chile

In Chile, as in most developing countries, barriers exist between the university and non-university sectors. Typically, a student who graduates from a non-university tertiary education institution, such as a vocational training institute, a technical institute, or a community college, has no choice but to enter the world of work. It is not possible to transfer directly to a university or even to a higher academic level in the non-university sector. It is also very difficult for these graduates to begin formal university studies after a few years of professional experience.

A recent initiative by the Universidad de Concepción aims to break this barrier. A two-year postsecondary vocational training center, a four-year technical institute, and the faculty of engineering of the university will be integrated, under a grant from the Competitive Quality Improvement Fund, supported by an ongoing Bank-financed higher education project. The curricula of all three institutions will be adjusted to allow for direct transfer of credits, and the vocational training center and the technical institute's qualifications will be recognized in determining admission to the faculty of engineering.

Source: Oxenham and others 2002.

Several significant issues need to be addressed before a country can move in this direction:

- *Establishing key competency and assessment standards.* Competency and assessment standards set up a universally recognized set of indicators against which all learning can be evaluated (see chapter 2). Many countries have established occupational and training standards for vocational education and training, and some are beginning to develop cross-national approaches and benchmark national standards to international requirements (Fretwell, Morgan, and Arjen 2001). Chile, Malaysia, the Philippines, and Romania have initiated projects with World Bank support to develop a system of national occupational competency and skill standards meeting the specific needs of their economies.
- *Recognizing nonformal learning.* An alternative approach to evaluating learning based on key competencies is to allow learners to demonstrate that their informal learning is equal to formal learning and to issue them certificates from formal learning institutions. Such a system is already in place in France (the *bilan de competence*) and the Republic of Korea (box 3.4). While the lure of a qualification may serve as an incentive for some learners, this approach leaves traditional "supply-side"

Box 3.4. The Republic of Korea's Flexible System of Recognizing Learning Outcomes

The Korean government has recently strengthened the Bachelor's Degree Examination Program for Self-Education. The program makes it possible to obtain a bachelor's degree through individual study without attending a regular college or university by passing the examination administered by the government. The program aims to realize the philosophy of lifelong learning, contribute to individual self-actualization, and develop society as a whole. A degree from this program is recognized in the same way as one obtained from a higher education institution. Degrees are offered in Korean, English, and Chinese language and literature; business administration; public administration; computer science; law; math; agriculture; nursing; early childhood education; and home economics.

Source: Bank staff working in the Republic of Korea.

---

institutions, which may or may not reflect the needs of the knowledge economy, in charge of the certification process.
* *Reducing tensions between formal and nonformal institutions.* Some formal institutions, particularly in higher education, may have difficulty accepting the idea that learning can take place outside a formal institution. These institutions, and related ministries of education, may feel threatened by nonformal learning approaches. For their part, nonformal institutions, such as traditional African apprenticeship systems, may fear that formal recognition may impose inappropriate standards. Enterprises may resist efforts to regulate and recognize their internal training.

Accrediting Institutions

Policymakers need to rethink the accreditation of institutions. This is because, on the one hand, the relationship between government and increasingly autonomous institutions is changing and, on the other, individuals are less and less likely to start and complete a qualification at a single institution over a single period of time. Reviewing accreditation mechanisms needs to establish a new link between the assessment of individual competencies and the evaluation of institutional capacity and performance.

The trend in OECD countries is toward accrediting institutions based on output or performance (such as graduation rates or the acquisition of knowledge and competencies) rather than inputs (such as the size of the faculty or the number of books in the library). This is also true in some developing countries. In Bangladesh, for example, private secondary schools must achieve certain pass rates on the university entrance examination to remain accredited (although this regulation is rarely enforced). In private (but not public) institutions of higher learning in Armenia, a certain percentage (currently 50 percent) of students must pass the final examination. Increasingly, funding of institutions is also based on performance.

A wide range of developing countries in Eastern Europe and Central Asia, Sub-Saharan Africa, and Latin America and the Caribbean have introduced independent assessment systems at the tertiary level (such systems remain rare in the Middle East and North Africa and in South Asia). Nigeria, for example, has had a system of regular accreditation assessments for 25 years. International experience suggests that while it is important to have a compulsory licensing process to ensure a minimum level of quality, regular accreditation and evaluation should be voluntary activities that institutions value as a way to improve their performance. Accreditation and evaluation can be encouraged through public information, financial incentives, and nonmonetary rewards (World Bank 2002c).

The fact that learners increasingly acquire skills and knowledge from multiple sources poses an even greater challenge to quality assurance, especially at the tertiary level. Currently, learners receive their degree or qualification from the last institution they attend, regardless of the contribution of that institution to the learner's overall learning gains. Where articulation agreements exist, including joint degree programs, both institutions award a degree, even though neither was responsible for providing all the learning gains. These new challenges remain contentious for industrial and developing countries.

To control quality and maintain accountability, many countries, including Chile, Colombia, France, and the United Kingdom, have established national standards and assessments at the primary and secondary education levels (Leithwood, Edge, and Jantzi 1999). It is important to distinguish between selection tests for access to the next level of education, which virtually all countries have, and tests at various stages of schooling certifying learning and providing for accountability, which are less common. South Africa, which had no national assessments under apartheid, introduced systemwide national assessments for grades 3, 6, and 9 to boost outcome-based, learner-centered education (Howie and others 2000). The assessments, which focus on achievement of defined learning outcomes, allow students to progress at their own rate and be assessed accordingly. They continually assess performance by monitoring portfolios, observation sheets, journals, project work, and assignments.

Accreditation and certification systems also help learners move easily and efficiently between different types and levels of learning. Several countries have developed national qualifications frameworks that assign qualifications from different institutions to a set of levels, with each level linked to competency standards. In this way learners can see what qualifications are of equal value and how they are sequenced (OECD 2002c). Since the mid-1980s several countries have been developing such frameworks. English-speaking nations (Australia, England, New Zealand, and Scotland) were the earliest to do so. More recently many other countries (China, Mauritius, Mexico, Trinidad and Tobago, South Africa, and Uganda) and regions (the Southern African Development Community and the Pacific Islands Forum) have developed or announced plans to develop frameworks (South Africa, Departments of Education and Labour 2002). A report on South Africa's experience (South Africa, Departments of Education and Labour 2002) suggests that most countries' national qualification frameworks have changed significantly, often following comprehensive reviews. It notes that debate is both an inevitable and positive part of the development process, since different traditions of education and training have to learn to speak to each other in common terms.

Frameworks for certifying qualifications come in various types, and all have evolved over time. (See box 3.5 for Namibia's experience.) Frameworks vary by the types of qualifications covered (occupational or vocational only, academic only, both); types of institutions included (university institutions only, all types of tertiary institutions); levels of qualifications involved (higher education, secondary education, first degree, postgraduate); fields of study (all vocational and academic fields, selected fields for which standards are developed); and how institutional participation is encouraged (voluntary, public funding available only for qualifications within the framework).

Perhaps the most developed example of a regional framework is that being established by the European Union (EU) to create a European Higher Education Area. The emphasis is on increasing mobility across undergraduate and graduate programs, in conjunction with the EU's European Credit Transfer System. Vocational and technical skills are not covered, nor are non-university institutions.

Making Information Available to Learners

Quality assurance systems must also make available information about the performance and offerings of learning providers. The Netherlands and the United Kingdom release information on assessment results by school, allowing parents to choose the public school they would like their child to attend.

Reliable information should be provided about programs offered by international providers. The fact that accreditation and evaluation

---

Box 3.5. The National Qualifications Framework in Namibia

In 1996 Namibia passed the Namibia Qualifications Authority (NQA) Act, intended to help transform education and training and recognize the learning that results rather than merely draw equivalences among different types of qualifications. To oversee the process, it established a 35-member council, made up of representatives of government ministries, labor unions, the private sector, and nongovernmental organizations. The council is chaired by the Permanent Secretary of the Ministry of Higher Education, Training, and Employment Creation.

The National Qualification Framework was intended to embrace all learning and all qualifications. The NQA Council adopted an eight-level framework, starting with compulsory schooling at level 1 and ending with doctorates at level 8. The Council approved 12 thematic areas, with the intention that a national standards-setting body would develop standards in each area following national consultation. Industrial or occupational groups are responsible for developing national standards in each area, based on a common set of steps developed by the Council. There has been considerable flexibility in developing the standards, which use international standards as the starting point.

The lack of an accreditation process for training providers has slowed implementation of the National Qualification Framework. The need for accreditation has become more urgent, especially given the presence of foreign providers. But funding for the Council's work has been inadequate, and the Council suffers from staff shortages.

Source: South Africa, Departments of Education and Labour 2002.

---

schemes of domestic institutions are weak in developing countries suggests that monitoring international providers will be difficult.

Effective grievance procedures and protections can be useful in ensuring quality and protecting against fraud. A survey in India revealed that 46 of 144 foreign providers (32 percent) advertising higher education programs in the newspapers were neither recognized nor accredited in their country of origin (World Bank 2002c). This raises the question of how learners can make informed choices about value. Hong Kong (China), India, and Singapore require that distance education offerings by international providers be subject to the same quality assurance procedures in their originating countries that on-campus courses in those countries face (World Bank 2002c). The development of international quality assurance mechanisms is another option.

Increasing Equity

Access to learning—and consequently learning achievement—is highly inequitably distributed in all societies. While the nature of the disadvantaged groups varies across countries, women, people in rural areas, ethnic minorities, the unemployed, people who work in the informal sector, and older workers generally have less opportunity to learn. The barriers these groups face are varied and in many cases individuals face multiple hurdles. For example, discrimination against women in the labor market reduces their incentive to invest in or complete education (Gill, Fluitman, and Dar 2001). Lack of access to schools within reasonable walking distance disadvantages rural children in Africa (World Bank 2001d). Employers tend to fund training of employees with higher levels of education and training (Hong and Batra 1995; O'Connell 1999).

The World Conference on Education for All, held in Jomtien, Thailand, in 1991 declared that all children should be able to complete primary education and that girls should have the same access as boys. People with only basic literacy and numeracy skills may have been able to function in mass production, agricultural, or informal economies (although disparities in education lead to social divisions). But, in the global knowledge economy, access to continuing education and training—that is, to lifelong learning—is a necessity for people who want to have high valued-added and secure well-paid jobs. A major focus of a government's policy for lifelong learning, therefore, must be improving the ability of disadvantaged groups and those with low educational attainment to access learning.

This report describes several ways this can be done. Changing the learning process, both by focusing on a broader range of competencies and transforming pedagogy, will enable more people to achieve the skills they need. Establishing accountability systems, often mediated by guidance and counseling systems, could help learners and their families make informed choices, not restricted by prejudiced or ill-informed word of mouth. Recognizing that informal and nonformal learning is a route to genuine skill acquisition enables people with less formal training to demonstrate the skills they have. Gender assessments in education have proved useful in identifying specific gender gaps in access to education and the use of knowledge as girls try to enter the labor market. They can help policymakers develop community- and country-specific mechanisms that address obstacles.

Another important policy tool is decentralization. The transfer of responsibilities from central ministries of education to local education authorities, communities, postsecondary institutions, and schools has become common. In Colombia, for example, decentralization reforms, designed with a focus on equity, have empowered poor communities through targeting mechanisms and voucher systems (Fiske 1996).

Conclusion

Refocusing government policy and reforming the policymaking system requires fundamental changes across a wide range of issues. These changes require a move toward a learner-centered system, the deployment of public resources and effort on learners with the greatest needs, and the creation of a flexible system of learning opportunities that responds to the different aptitudes, circumstances, and goals of learners. Making a lifelong learning system a reality will depend on giving people, enterprises, and communities the resources they need to pursue their learning goals—the subject of the next chapter.

4
Options for Financing Lifelong Learning

Modern economies require that people invest in the acquisition of knowledge, skills, and information throughout most of their lives.

Gary S. Becker, Nobel Laureate, Economic Sciences, 1992

Providing more and better education and training opportunities over a lifetime will require increased expenditures, although resources will also need to be used more efficiently and in different ways. These expenditures cannot be met solely from public sources. A creative partnership between the private and public sectors is required.

The financing of lifelong learning requires public spending on levels of education for which social returns exceed private returns (such as basic education) and increased private spending on investments that yield higher private returns (such as most higher and continuing education). Government intervention beyond the basic levels should target learners from low-income backgrounds.

This chapter focuses on the government's role in financing learning. As noted in chapter 3, governments also need to perform other roles to ensure the effective operation of a learner-centered lifelong learning system. Enhancing the choices available to potential learners by increasing the information flow about and among education institutions is critical for ensuring the effective use of resources.

The Growing Need to Support Lifelong Learning

Moving toward a lifelong learning system is costly in developing countries because participation rates are low at all levels and the quality of education is often poor. Average gross enrollment rates are lowest in low-income countries, where they averaged 97 percent at the primary, 46 percent at the secondary, and 8 percent at the tertiary level in 1998. These figures fail to capture the wastage in schools, especially in countries in which delayed entry, repetition, and drop-out rates are high. Marginalized populations are usually the poor, women, ethnic and religious minorities, and people living in rural or remote areas.

It is estimated that in 2003 one out of every five children between the ages of 6 and 11 in developing countries—an estimated 113 million children—is not in school (http://www1.worldbank.org/education/adultoutreach/). In 2000 an estimated 40 percent of the out-of-school population lived in Sub-Saharan Africa, another 40 percent lived in South Asia, and more than 15 percent lived in the Middle East and North Africa. Sixty percent are girls (UNESCO 2000).

The education level of most adults in developing countries remains too low to enable them to participate effectively in a global economy. Some 600 million women and 300 million men remain illiterate. Adults average just 0.8 years of formal education in Mali and Niger, 1.1 years in Mozambique and Ethiopia, 2.0 years in Nepal, and 2.5 years in Bangladesh (World Bank 2002a). Greater investments in adult education, especially for women, are needed to eliminate illiteracy and build human capital. With such low levels of basic skills, however, the priority for these countries remains universal basic education.

Many industrial countries have set targets for lifelong learning. Meeting these targets would require large increases in spending beyond the 5 percent of GDP these countries currently spend on average on public education (OECD 2001a). The OECD (2000d) argues for increasing the benefits and reducing the costs of education so that individuals, enterprises, and societies invest in lifelong learning.

Even the most optimistic scenarios for achieving universal primary completion by 2015 suggest that Sub-Saharan Africa would require a sevenfold increase in foreign assistance for primary education (World Bank 2002a). Sub-Saharan African countries would need to allocate nearly 4 percent of GNP to secondary schooling alone to achieve 60 percent gross enrollment; achieving 100 percent secondary gross enrollment would require spending of more than 6 percent of GNP (Lewin and Caillods 2001).

Improving quality will prove even more costly for developing countries. While the bulk of spending on education is based on local costs, other inputs, especially computers, laboratories, and Internet access, are priced internationally.

Public sources account for more than half of education spending in developing countries as a group, and most governments spend 10–20 percent of their budgets on education (3–7 percent of GNP). Public finance is thus inadequate to extend lifelong learning opportunities to all.

In addition to public spending, individuals and companies contribute to education, especially at postcompulsory levels. Global spending on education is more than $2 trillion, or 5 percent, of world GDP (Moe, Bailey, and Lau 1999). The private sector accounts for about 20 percent of this spending, often in the form of fees, donations, sponsorships, and loans and investments made by philanthropists, learners, parents, corporations, lending agencies, communities, NGOs, and cultural organizations. In addition, about $2 trillion in earnings are forgone each year to pursue education. This investment is financed by parents or by learners who accept below-market wages as apprentices or interns while in training in return for higher returns later. Evidence from 41 countries suggests that private spending makes up a larger proportion of total direct education spending in developing countries (25 percent) than in Western Europe (12 percent), suggesting a potential equity issue.

Wage differentials—which provide an incentive to invest in skills—are widening in the knowledge economy. Narrowing the wage differentials among workers with different levels of education is expected to be very costly—perhaps as high as $1.66 trillion in the United States alone (Heckman, Roselius, and Smith 1994). Providing lifelong learning opportunities will require increased spending on education and training (by both the public and the private sector), but building in incentive schemes (capital accumulation) could reduce the investment needed.

Private direct expenditures on education are substantial in some countries and are on the rise (figure 4.1). For all education subsectors combined, private direct spending averaged 45 percent of all spending in

Figure 4.1. Proportion of Private Funding Spent on Educational Institutions in Selected Countries, 1990s (percent)

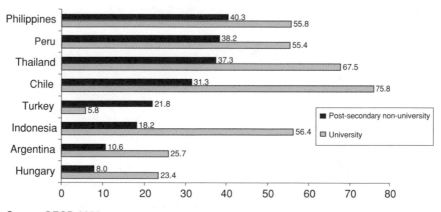

Source: OECD 2000a.

Chile, 24 percent in Ghana, 37 percent in Indonesia, and 57 percent in Uganda in the early to mid-1990s.

Between 1995 and 2000, only 15 percent of enrollment growth in higher education was publicly funded in Brazil. This trend is likely to continue there, as enrollments are expected to more than double, from 2.1 million in 2000 to more than 5 million in 2008 (Klor de Alva 2001). In China, with its massive need for skilled labor, the demand for learning is increasing, but lack of spaces at higher education institutions meant that almost 95 percent of high school graduates were denied entry to universities in 1995. Families use their savings to send their children to private tertiary institutions (Klor de Alva 2001), but additional resources are needed.

Principles for Financing Lifelong Learning

Given the rising demand for—and expenditures on—learning, what principles should guide policy decisions about the balance between public and private resources for financing different learning opportunities? The overarching principle is that the system should promote learning throughout the lifetime. Achieving this goal will take time, even for industrial countries. Even countries that need to make substantial progress in basic education need to ensure that any system of financing will be sustainable in the long run, as lifelong learning demands increase.

Several financing mechanisms are consistent with the principles outlined here. Before choosing a mechanism, policymakers need to study its impact on the labor market and on the decisions people make about where to work and when to learn.

Four principles underlie investments in lifelong learning:

- All learners should master basic competencies.
- Learners should be responsible for their own learning.
- Governments must be committed to promoting equity.
- A lifelong learning system should promote efficiency in education and labor markets.

All Learners Should Master Basic Competencies

The foundation of education for the knowledge economy is the set of basic knowledge and competencies outlined in chapter 2. In addition to providing the tools for effective engagement in the knowledge economy and society, these skills are associated with high social returns. Governments should finance or guarantee opportunities for all to acquire this basic set of competencies. These opportunities include primary and lower secondary education for young people as well as adult education for people who missed out on an effective education the first time around. They could also include early childhood interventions.

As countries approach universal basic education, they will need to expand lower and upper secondary education. Enrollment in postcompulsory secondary education is relatively low in many developing and even middle-income countries. The availability of this level of schooling is imperative for providing incentives to learners who complete basic education and for preparing workers for the knowledge economy as well as for additional education and training.

Countries will need to expand secondary education in a cost-effective and sustainable manner. One objective is to ensure that learners not likely to benefit from traditional secondary schooling are provided with alternatives.

Innovative ways of increasing secondary school enrollment include offering selective scholarships and targeted vouchers. Scholarships for girls in Bangladesh have increased higher secondary school enrollment rates (Jeria and Hovde 2002). Targeted vouchers allowed learners from lower socioeconomic groups to attend secondary schools in Colombia (Angrist and others 2001). The scheme was also cost-effective. Another approach would be to increase cost recovery at the upper secondary level among those who can pay and to provide targeted scholarships for those who cannot.

To provide adequate secondary schooling and ensure that the system is sustainable, policymakers should also consider providing education through the private sector, through distance learning, and on-line. To facilitate alternative delivery of secondary schooling, Japan and the Republic of Korea have for years used tax incentives to privatize upper secondary education (Yoon 2002; Japan, MESSC 1991). In Burkina Faso, where the government cannot sustain the recurrent costs of a significant expansion in secondary school enrollment, partnerships are being fostered with the private sector to provide good-quality secondary education (Maman and Scobie 2002). The initiatives include constructing three lower secondary schools in underserved areas and delegating their management to nonpublic organizations at no recurrent cost to the government; providing lease financing for the construction of 10 private schools to be operated and paid for on easy terms by private sector operators or self-financed municipalities, with a transfer of ownership to the nonpublic operator after payment in full; and jointly constructing 160 additional classrooms at existing private schools.

Reallocating public resources would also help. In many countries in which secondary education is underfunded, higher education is overfunded. Adopting alternative financing mechanisms for higher education would allow more resources to be redeployed toward expanding secondary education enrollments. Other efficiency-enhancing measures include using teachers and facilities more intensively.

Learners Should Be Responsible for Their Own Learning

For learning beyond the core set of competencies, learners, employers, and in some cases society should be principally responsible for learning decisions. Learners should be responsible for deciding what to learn and when to continue learning. The public sector role is to ensure that risk-adverse and liquidity- or wealth-constrained learners and companies do not underinvest in learning. It can do so by providing financial incentives and making sure that relevant and timely information is disseminated.

Governments Must Be Committed to Promoting Equity

Certain socioeconomic groups displaced by new technologies become unemployed and marginalized from educational opportunities. They require targeted efforts by governments. Current public expenditure disproportionately favors higher-income groups in many countries, including the poorest countries (figure 4.2). On average in developing countries the poorest 20 percent receive about one-fifth of the primary education subsidy, about one-tenth of the secondary education subsidy, and a tiny percentage of the tertiary level subsidy. Services in poorer rural communities are generally inferior to those provided at urban schools (Castro-Leal and others 1999; see also Li, Steele, and Glewwe 1999).

Figure 4.2. Distribution of Public Expenditures by Income Quintile in Selected Countries (percent)

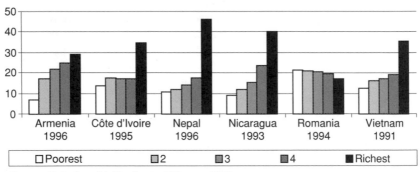

Source: Data from Li, Steele, and Glewwe 1999.

A Lifelong Learning System Should Promote Efficiency in Education and Labor Markets

Policies for financing lifelong learning should enhance the choices available to learners, expand the information available to them, and increase competition in the learning marketplace. The impact of a policy on the labor market should also be taken into account. Financing mechanisms should be analyzed in terms of their contribution to work effort and labor market decisions by individuals.

Policy Options for Financing Learning beyond the Core Competencies

Learning beyond the core knowledge and competencies is funded with two types of financing components: cost-sharing schemes and government subsidies. Education savings accounts, private sector loans, human capital contracts, government-guaranteed student loans, individual development accounts, vouchers and entitlements, grants, tax credits, and other mechanisms all include one or both of these components (table 4.1). Most countries use a variety of instruments (box 4.1)

Cost-sharing, especially in advanced vocational programs and at the tertiary level, promotes efficiency, but without other policy measures such a system largely excludes the poor. Innovative cost-sharing schemes such as income-contingent student loans and human capital contracts are currently largely conceptual. Most cannot be implemented in low-income countries because of the lack of necessary institutional arrangements. Effectively targeted public subsidies can promote equity, but they may not be sustainable on a large scale.

Cost-Sharing Schemes

In cost-sharing schemes learners are expected to pay for at least part of the cost of their learning. This approach is commonly advocated in higher education on grounds of efficiency and equity (Barr 2001; Johnstone 2001). Cost-sharing is efficient because learners bear the marginal costs of their education. They therefore make better (less wasteful) choices and study harder. Cost-sharing is equitable in theory because it asks those who benefit from education to pay for it. However, if cost-sharing schemes are not introduced carefully, they can make it difficult for low-income learners to obtain additional education. Four main cost-sharing instruments are traditional loans, human capital contracts, the graduate tax, and income-contingent loans (for details, see Palacios 2002).

Table 4.1. Main Instruments for Financing Direct Costs of Lifelong Learning

Who ultimately pays	Who finances	Collection	Repayment terms	Instrument
Learner	Learner	n.a.	n.a.	Education savings account
	Private sector	Private sector	Fixed	Private sector loan
			Combined	Private sector income-contingent loan
			Variable	Human capital contract
		Public sector	Fixed	Government-guaranteed student loan
			Combined	Institutional income-contingent loan
			Variable	Institutional human capital contract
	Public sector	Private sector	Fixed	Privately collected public sector loan
			Combined	
			Variable	
		Public sector	Fixed	Public sector loan
			Combined	Public sector income-contingent loan
			Variable	Graduate tax
		Community	Variable	Individual development account
Employer	Private sector	n.a.	Variable	On-the-job training
				Training levy
	Public sector	Public sector	Variable	Employer's graduate tax
Government (taxpayer)	n.a.	n.a.	n.a.	Direct funding
			n.a.	Vouchers and entitlements
			n.a.	Grants
			n.a.	Interest subsidy on loans
			n.a.	Tax credits

n.a. Not applicable.
Source: Based on Palacios 2002.

Box 4.1. Financing Postsecondary Education and Training in Chile

Chile uses several instruments to finance education and training at the postsecondary level, including direct funding from the state, vouchers, directed subsidies, tax rebates, and income-contingent loans. The system now finances nontraditional learners as well. The main source of funds for universities is transfers from the state. Other sources of public funding include an institutional development fund and a fund for the development of priority areas, to which all universities have access. These funds represent 12 percent of public transfers.

Different treatment of traditional and new higher education institutions (most of which are private) makes tuition much lower at traditional institutions. The difference in fees is not compensated for by financial help to learners in the form of grants or loans. As a result, financing an education at a traditional school, at which courses are longer and the opportunity costs of not working higher, is less of a burden than doing so at a nontraditional institution, putting low-income learners at a disadvantage. Thus although 30 percent of high school graduates in Chile went on to higher education institutions in 1999, 85 percent of students at the new private universities came from the two highest socioeconomic quintiles.

The second most important type of public funds is grants to learners from underprivileged backgrounds. The grants, which are distributed according to various criteria, represented 27 percent of state funding of higher education in 1999.

Indirect fiscal contributions, the third source of public funds, are similar to a voucher scheme. The amount each institution receives depends on the number of first-year students who are top performers on the entrance examination. The result is competition among institutions to attract the best learners, who usually come from the highest-income families (because of the very high correlation between test scores and parental income). Indirect fiscal contributions represented 10 percent of public spending on higher education in 1999.

The government offers a tax rebate for staff training programs. The scheme allows firms to set training costs of up to 1 percent of annual payroll against corporate tax payments. A firm can also use 10 percent of the rebate to pay for a diagnosis of its training needs and 15 percent to run a training department.

Chile also uses cost-sharing schemes to finance higher education. The two most important are the university credit and the Corfo credit.

(continued)

Box 4.1. (*Continued*)

The university credit is an income-contingent loan in which the learner pays the lower of a fixed payment or 5 percent of income. The real interest rate on the loan is 2 percent, and interest is accrued from the moment the loan is made. This credit is collected by the universities and has had low recovery rates, averaging 59 percent in 1998 for traditional schools. The Corfo credit is offered by banks, which can charge a maximum real interest rate of 9 percent. All credits have a maximum repayment period of 15 years. Neither credit is adequate to satisfy the demand for financing education, particularly for learners from low-income backgrounds and learners pursuing risky careers.

Source: Camhi and Latuf 2000.

Mortgage-Type Loans

To make cost-sharing more equitable, many countries have introduced student finance systems. The most popular instrument—traditional mortgage-type loans—are likely to be offered only to families who already have enough assets to serve as collateral—that is, precisely those who need financial aid the least.

Traditional student loans have been collected by the state, by private banks, and by universities. Collection has been poor or costly where the taxing power of the state has not been used as a last resort to collect the loans. In some cases, as in the Philippines (box 4.2), poor collection rates have caused such schemes to operate at a loss.

Box 4.2. The Philippines' Financial Aid Scheme

The Philippines developed a financial aid scheme in the 1980s to provide financial support to students attending public tertiary institutions. The system provides traditional mortgage-type loans, which are managed by a government agency. The amount of the loan, set at about $1,000 in the 1970s, was never adjusted for inflation, making it worth about $141 today. The system enrolls only 2,000 students a year; due to high administration costs and low repayment rates, it produces a loss. Proposals to reform the system envision making it more responsive to the needs of students while at the same time recovering from students part of the costs of their education.

Source: Palacios 2002.

Human Capital Contracts

A human capital contract is a contract in which students agree to pay a percentage of their income for a specified period after graduation in exchange for funds to finance their education. Originally proposed by Milton Friedman (Friedman and Kuznets 1945; Friedman 1955), the idea of such contracts has re-emerged in recent years. The development of financial markets since the 1980s has created favorable conditions for a private initiative to invest in human capital.

An essential characteristic of human capital contracts is that investors determine the percentage of future income that students have to commit, which could vary depending on the type of learning undertaken and the investor's judgment about the borrower's likely future income. From an efficiency perspective, optimal results are achieved when market forces determine the percentage of income that learners have to commit and externalities are covered by public subsidy. For the outcomes to optimize social welfare, distributional considerations must also be taken into account by targeting public subsidies in order to achieve equity.

Implementation of human capital contracts is constrained by the difficulty of obtaining information on learners, the need for a developed tax collection agency, and the problem of adverse selection (Palacios 2002). No market for effectively trading human capital currently exists, but that could change (boxes 4.3 and 4.4).

Graduate Taxes

The idea of the graduate tax gained popularity during the 1960s and again during the 1980s. Graduate taxes are not in operation anywhere in the world.

A graduate tax taxes all earnings, without discriminating between earnings due to additional education and those due to other factors, such as ability or industry. As a result, the graduate tax creates a disincentive for people who would have obtained high earnings without education to pursue additional training. In addition, high-earning graduates would pay far more than they borrowed (even allowing for interest on the loan amount), raising fairness concerns.

Another concern with the graduate tax is what Barr (2001) calls the Mick Jagger effect. Mick Jagger attended the London School of Economics and Political Science for two semesters before dropping out and starting his career as a rock musician. Barr questions whether it would be fair to tax Jagger for attending school when his education presumably had nothing to do with his financial success.

Box 4.3. Trading Human Capital Contracts: MyRichUncle

Established in 1999, MyRichUncle is the world's sole provider of human capital contracts. It represents the securitization of human capital (Davis and Meyer 2000). As of January 2002 the firm had provided financial support to 65 people.

MyRichUncle offers financing to people who want to study in exchange for a fixed percentage (1–5 percent) of their income over a specified period of time (typically 10 years for graduate students and 15 years for undergraduate students). The percentage of income the borrower pays depends on the amount provided, the school attended, and the course of study, among other factors.

One potential problem is selecting learners. Because high-income earners may see MyRichUncle's offer as expensive, they may not take it. As a result, at least in theory, learners with lower incomes are more likely to participate, reducing the average payments that MyRichUncle can expect to receive. MyRichUncle responds to these concerns by stating that it can distinguish between high- and low-income potential learners and set rates accordingly. It claims that applications do not reflect any bias toward learners with low-income potential. People who have studied the company's business model also question the firm's capacity to collect payments.

MyRichUncle has been receiving attention from the media, and the firm is receiving a growing number of applications. It is too early to tell if it will succeed. Regardless of the company's performance, it is opening a new path for financing education that can transform the way other private institutions and governments think about this alternative. The fact that the company has customers shows that there is demand for human capital contracts even in the United States, where resources for financing education are widely available.

Source: Palacios 2002.

Box 4.4. Investing in the Future Earning Capacity of a Rock Star: Bowie Bonds

Bowie Bonds, issued in 1997 by the Pullman Group, allowed the singer David Bowie to obtain funds in exchange for a percentage of his income from royalties and concerts. Issue of the bonds indicates that there are investors willing to invest in the future earnings capacity of an individual. The Bowie Bonds opened up a path for others to trade future earnings, probably in the highest-earning professions.

Source: Palacios 2002.

Income-Contingent Repayment Schemes

Several countries have implemented income-contingent repayment schemes (box 4.5). These schemes satisfy fairness concerns, since learners end up paying less than the value of the loan if they have low incomes during the repayment period. Unlike human capital contracts, income-contingent repayment schemes do not attract immediate private funding; in the short run, the additional resources come from the public purse.

The collection mechanism contributes significantly to the success of any loan scheme. Australia's continued success with the HECS is due largely to the income tax system. Countries with less efficient tax collection regimes have worked out alternative mechanisms. Namibia uses the social security system, thereby keeping marginal costs of collection low (box 4.6).

All of these cost-sharing mechanisms have been designed for young students entering higher education for the first time and studying full-time. But there is no reason in principle why these schemes could not be made available to part-time and older learners. The United States has revised the eligibility requirement in terms of number of hours studied, a change that would allow part-time learners to access financing options. Financing nontraditional learners increases the risk of nonpayment, however, because the period of repayment is shorter for older learners. It also raises marginal administration costs, since nontraditional learners take fewer courses (and therefore borrow less money) and are enrolled over a longer period of time (and therefore begin repayments years after the loan is made).

Subsidization Mechanisms

A variety of subsidization mechanisms could be used to finance lifelong learning (table 4.2). Demand-side financing includes a range of interventions that channel public funds for education and training (provided by public or private institutions) to learners or their families (box 4.7). The focus is on putting the resources in the hands of those who demand education rather than those who supply it. The aim is to reduce the constraints that prevent learners from attending school or continuing their education in other ways and to provide an incentive for institutions to respond to learner needs.

Some private initiatives support both basic education and lifelong learning skills. The Africa Educational Trust (www.iprt.org/africa_educational_trust.htm), a charitable organization, operates the Somali Educational Incentives for Girls and Young Men (SEIGYM), which provides educational vouchers to enable disadvantaged girls and young ex-militia

Box 4.5. Australia's Higher Education Contribution Scheme (HECS)

Australia's Higher Education Contribution Scheme (HECS) aims to eliminate the inequity of free higher education, increase the resources available to expand the supply of higher education, and improve access for learners from low-income backgrounds. Under HECS every learner pays a fee for attending a higher education institution. The fee can be paid immediately at a 25 percent discount, or it can be financed through an income-contingent loan. Repayments of the loan are made through the tax collection agency and depend on income, with the percentage paid ranging from 3 percent to 6 percent. In 1996 learners had to pay $1,900, regardless of the field of study. The amount was increased that year and differential fees ranging from $3,300 to $5,500 applied, depending on the field of study. The interest rate on the loan is adjusted to equal the rate of inflation, making the real rate of interest zero.

HECS brought in $80 million in 1989, the year of its inception, and generated $700 million in 2001. The cost of collection is about 1.7 percent of the value of payments. The resources HECS has brought in have allowed the state to increase the supply of higher education by 60 percent. Participation by the lowest income quartile, middle half, and top quartile has increased in absolute terms since 1989.

HECS' success is due, at least in part, to two key factors: a developed tax collection agency and the discount for up-front payments. The successful widespread collection of payments to HECS would be virtually impossible without a developed tax collection agency or an equivalent institution that has information on learners' incomes and can collect payments from them. The discount that learners receive if they pay up front was the key to the program having had such an impact from the first year. A lesson for revenue generation is that learners should always have the alternative to pay up front.

The greatest limitation of HECS is that the government has not been able to sell to the private sector the $6 billion that learners owe. The primary reason is fear of a political change that would wipe out the obligation of learners to pay back their loans. Not being able to use capital from the private sector limits the financing of higher education, or any other investment, to current resources. The inability to tap private funds might prevent increases in the supply of higher education in countries facing more pressing budget constraints.

Sources: Chapman 2001; Johnstone 2001; Johnstone and Aemero 2001; Andrews 1997.

Box 4.6. Namibia's Income-Contingent Loan Scheme

Namibia finances higher education through an income-contingent loan scheme. It uses the recently established social security system, rather than the tax collection agency, to collect payments from learners.

The system consists of two types of loans, one covering tuition and the other covering living and other expenses. The first type of loan is universally available and provides $700 in financing. The second type of loan is offered only to some borrowers, who receive $1,000. These amounts can be renewed each year as the learner progresses. In addition to the loan, the package can include a grant. For loans available to all learners, a discount of 10 percent is granted to those who pay their fees when commencing their courses. In general, the amount available for loans depends on the government's budget. Repayments are income contingent and can cost as much as 10 percent of postgraduate salary, with payments starting when the learner reaches a minimum weekly income of about $17 a week. The loan carries an interest of 1–2 percent above inflation, and there is no upper limit to the repayment period.

Namibia's scheme was designed in 1996 and established shortly thereafter. Little is known about outcome, but two important points can be made. First, contrary to expectations, income-contingent loans were widely accepted by learners. Their acceptance is attributed to the fact that both learners and institutional student welfare officers were closely involved in the design of the program. Second, countries can consider sources for collecting payments other than the tax collection agency (although it is still early to tell whether the social security system will be a good collector of payments and collection will be cost-efficient).

Source: Nicholls 1998.

---

men who are unable to benefit from normal schooling to attend special afternoon or evening lessons. The project issues vouchers to the students to help them pay for courses of their choice in literacy, numeracy, small-scale industry, and computer training.

Student loans can help defray costs to the government and allow a greater number of students to receive higher education. The World Bank–financed Mexico Higher Education Financing Project promotes equity and quality in the university system. A private sector student loan program helps improve access to private education for learners who are academically able but financially needy (World Bank 1998f).

Table 4.2. Selected Options for Financing Lifelong Learning

Instrument	Description	Main variables	Strengths	Weaknesses	Examples
Cost-sharing mechanisms					
Traditional loan	Fixed payments, specific period of time	Amount borrowed, interest rate, repayment period	Implementation relatively easy, instrument easy to understand	Requires collateral, therefore benefits wealthier more; not attractive to students as the terms of repayment do not adjust to capacity to pay; poor collection record	Numerous
Human capital contract	Student commits part of future earnings for fixed period in exchange for capital for financing education	Percentage of future income to be repaid, repayment period, collection of payments	Creates a market for investing in skills, decreases risks of default, offers measure of expected value of education, adjusts payments to earnings capacity, equitable	Information on individuals difficult to obtain, requires developed tax collection (or similar) agency, adverse selection, could create disincentive to work	MyRichUncle (United States)
Income-contingent loan	Collects percentage of income until value of loan repaid or maximum repayment period reached	Percentage of future income to be repaid, repayment period	Decreases risk to individuals, eliminates default risk, equitable, promotes incentive to study	Requires developed tax collection (or similar) agency but (see box 4.6) does not fully reflect expected value of education	Australia, Ghana, Hungary, Namibia, New Zealand, Sweden, United Kingdom

(continued)

Graduate tax	Tax on learner's future earnings	Tax rate	Universal, flexible, payments throughout lifetime of individual	Payments throughout lifetime, requires developed tax collection (or similar) agency, all earnings treated equally, could create disincentive to study, no private initiative	
Subsidization mechanisms					
Voucher (and other demand-side financing mechanisms)	Channels public funds for public and private education to individuals or their families	Costs of schooling, target population/schooling level, demand-side financing	Funding based on demand/enrollments, efficient, equitable, quality of schooling	Need to market, funds could be misused, may not be sustainable	Bangladesh, Chile, Guatemala, Netherlands, Pakistan, Sweden
Entitlement	Voucher and loan combination	Amount of entitlement (voucher and loan), cofinance amount, repayment terms	Targets individuals based on income and motivation, helps build individual's assets, sustainable	Need to market, funds could be misused	Theoretical, but U.S. GI Bill and Brazil's Bolsa Escola (box 4.9) comes close; numerous student loan schemes

(continued)

Table 4.2. (*Continued*)

Instrument	Description	Main variables	Strengths	Weaknesses	Examples
Subsidization mechanisms (Continued)					
Individual Learning Account	Incentives for investing in education and training	Individual subsidy, cofinance amount, type of training	Individual responsibility, private sector participation	Funds could be misused, need to market, may not be sustainable	Netherlands, Scandia (Sweden (public and private initiatives), Spain, Sweden (proposed), Switzerland, United Kingdom (suspended)
Education Savings Account	Incentives for savings for education and training	Individual subsidy, cofinance amount, tax discount	Individual responsibility, builds assets, targeted	Need to market, may not be sustainable	Canada
Learning tax credit	Taxes reduced in proportion to spending on approved education and training	Tax discount, spending maximum	Individual responsibility, private sector participation	Lack of equity, may not be sustainable	United States

Box 4.7. Financing Education with Demand-Side Mechanisms in Denmark

Denmark uses several demand-side financing mechanisms to promote choice and efficiency. Choice and competitive funding characterize the higher education system. Basic and secondary schools are financed based on student demand, through a funding formula that allocates resources directly to institutions based on enrollments.

To provide equal opportunities for people 18 and older to participate in education regardless of socioeconomic background, the Danish government has taken over the responsibility of supporting students. It does so through the State Education Grant and Loan Scheme. Students enrolled at institutions of higher learning are entitled to 70 monthly grant and loan disbursements (vouchers). The vouchers are calculated as the normal maximum stipulated duration of a tertiary education course of 58 months (corresponding to a total of 5 years of study) plus an accepted delay of 12 months. Students can use their vouchers for one long study program or one or more shorter programs. They are free to change from one course to another at the same or another educational institution (provided they are admitted). Courses need not be taken consecutively.

To improve efficiency and allocate resources on an outcome-based basis, in 1990 Denmark adopted an innovative financing system known as a taximeter, or activity-based, allocation system. Originally introduced for upper secondary technical college level and business colleges, the system was expanded to include private primary, lower secondary schools, tertiary education, adult vocational training, "folk" high schools, and production schools (schools based on production of goods as part of the learning process). Today it is the principal mechanism in Denmark for channeling to institutions the funds they need to manage their operating and capital costs.

Under the system, individual educational institutions remain free to set their own priorities for allocating funds without being hampered by central educational frameworks. Schools receive grants based on the number of learners, their age, the seniority of teachers, and school activities. They receive four kinds of grants: a basic grant, a teaching grant, an operational grant, and a building grant to cover rent, interest, debt servicing, and maintenance.

Incentives to make the education system and lifelong learning more effective are strategically designed by putting the institutions under competitive pressure using two mechanisms. First, as education

(continued)

Box 4.7. (*Continued*)

consumers have autonomy to select their providers and providers are paid only for the number of learners enrolled, the institutions have an incentive to provide good-quality education in order to attract learners. Second, by allowing educational institutions to retain any excess in taximeter rates over actual costs and forcing them to pay any costs in excess of the taximeter rates, the system encourages institutions to find more efficient ways to offer education and training.

Funding for learners is limited to the period of active study, over a continuous period or with breaks. Funding for institutions becomes available only when learners pass their examinations.

Two features of this system stand out. First, because taximeter payments are guaranteed to approved institutions as long as they enroll students, they can enroll large numbers. To address the associated budget uncertainty, in 1999 the authorities agreed to create a reserve of 1–2 percent of the total allocation for the scheme to cover unforeseen surges in enrollments. Second, if the taximeter rates are adjusted too frequently to take account of efficiency gains, providers may have less incentive to pursue efficiency-enhancing innovations; if taximeter rates are adjusted too slowly, there may be a loss in overall efficiency to the extent that some providers continue to use less efficient methods. Although the government has no intention of recapturing the "profits" realized by institutions whose actual costs are below the taximeter rates, there may be some adjustment in rates to improve the overall efficiency of the system.

Sources: Anthony 2001; OECD 1999, 2001c; Patrinos 2001b.

Policy Options for Financing Training and Nontraditional Learning

As learners pursue learning throughout their lifetimes, they will require more flexible financing options. A financial aid package for each learner consisting of financial grants and a voucher (both means-tested), some student loans, and some expected private contribution from the learner, his or her parents, or both, holds the greatest potential for meeting these lifelong learning needs (Oosterbeek 1998). The relative importance of each of these elements would vary over the learner's lifetime.

Providing such a package—in combination with loans for high-income, highly motivated learners—could support an effective and sustainable mode of financing based on two principal parameters: the income level and the motivation level of the student. Such a package would build on components that have been successfully implemented in developing countries and elsewhere. At the primary level the package would consist only of grants. For secondary education, higher education, and adult learning, the package could include a mix of schemes.

Payroll Levies

Payroll levies are often used to finance occupational training (box 4.8). In some countries, including Brazil and France, they are used to finance civics education. There are two general approaches. In the first the government levies a payroll tax on employers. The central government or a quasi-government agency then conducts training using funds from the levy. In some countries, such as Nigeria, this model has encountered problems, because it tends to create large, self-perpetuating bureaucracies. Some countries, including the United Kingdom, have stopped imposing such levies.

An alternative model is one in which employers manage the levy. In this model, in place in France, Hungary, and Malaysia, employers who

---

Box 4.8. Training Levy Schemes in Brazil, France, and Malaysia

Brazil: As they do in many Latin American countries, national training organizations in Brazil receive payroll tax funds to provide training for workers in enterprises and to sponsor apprentices on a cost-sharing basis. The level of financing, which is under review, is currently about 2.9 percent of wages. There is some concern that the organizations are overfunded, and options for refining the system are being discussed.

France: Since 1971 French enterprises with more than 10 employees have had to devote 1.5 percent of gross payroll to training their staff, either internally or by contracting with an external training provider. Enterprises that choose to train their employees themselves do so within the framework of an annual or multiyear training plan. The employer can choose the type of training and designate which employees should attend it. This system is believed to have contributed to a large increase in training in enterprises and to have helped ensure equity and access to training by workers in small enterprises.

Malaysia: The 1992 Human Resources Development Act instituted a human resources development levy of 1 percent of the total monthly basic wages or fixed allowances of the employees. It currently covers firms with 10 or more employees and represents one of the major streams for financing training in Malaysia.

Source: Fretwell and Colombano 2000.

document that they have provided training to their employees are for-given part of the levy. One problem with this approach is that companies can use the funds for other activities and charge them to training. More-over, even these levies can create entrenched bureaucracies. Levies can also drive up the cost of labor. Brazil, for example, has multiple payroll taxes, including training levies, which amount to 80–110 percent of net wages. The net impact of these levies also remains unclear, as the policy may encourage employers to provide more internal training than they otherwise would have.

Entitlement Schemes

Entitlement schemes embrace different types of learning (including on-the-job training) over a learner's lifetime (Levin and Schütze 1983; Levin 2002). Learners are entitled to receive from the government an amount to spend on education. The funds can be used in a wide variety of accredited institutions, and they are adjusted for inflation during the learner's life-time. The entitlement consists of a voucher and a loan. The voucher por-tion can be used to target groups of students. To facilitate learners' choices, the government provides information and increases the efficiency of the market. The subsidy/loan package is very similar to the U.S. GI Bill, which financed both college education and adult vocational training for millions of veterans after World War II and for a period thereafter (Dohmen 2000).

Education vouchers are typically used to finance primary and sec-ondary education, but they are also being used to finance preschool and higher education. Several countries also provide them for training. Paraguay has used vouchers to finance training since 1995 (Botelho and Goldmark 2000). Kenya provides training vouchers to entrepreneurs in the *jua kali* (cottage industry) sector through the Micro-Small Enterprise Training Fund (Middleton, Ziderman, and Adams 1993). Five of Austria's eight provinces provide training vouchers cofinanced by the provincial government and voucher recipients (West, Sparkes, and Balabanov 2000). Private and company-sponsored voucher schemes are also in place. In the United Kingdom the Ford Employee Development and Assistance Pro-gram has been operating since 1989 (West, Sparkes, and Balabanov 2000). It functions as a voucher that allows employees to receive education and training. (For more information on training vouchers, see Ziderman 2001.)

Asset-Building Schemes

Schemes that enable learners to build human capital and financial assets have increased primary school enrollment and completion in Brazil (box 4.9), and they have been adopted in other countries. In the past few

---

Box 4.9. Increasing School Enrollment through Stipends in Brazil: The Bolsa Escola Program

In 1995 the municipality of Brasilia launched the innovative Bolsa Escola program with the goal of increasing educational attainment and reducing the incidence of child labor. Bolsa Escola aims to break the vicious cycle of poverty and low educational attainment in Brazil. The relevance of this program for lifelong learning is based on its use of voucher-like instruments that include grants to offset the opportunity cost of attending school.

The program also includes a savings program that creates an incentive for staying in school. The school savings program deposits money into the account of each child whose family is a beneficiary of the scholarship program if the child is promoted to the next grade. Half of the amount deposited can be withdrawn when the child reaches the fifth grade. Withdrawals can be made again upon successful completion of the eighth grade and secondary school. A similar program in Mexico, Progresa, has reduced child labor, increased educational attainment, and improved health and nutrition for the poor (www.progresa.gob.mx).

Source: World Bank 2001a.

---

years, important demand-side financing initiatives in education have been implemented in several countries. These programs include *Progresa/ Oportunidades* in Mexico, scholarships and food for education in Bangladesh, scholarships for girls in Guatemala, and secondary school scholarships in Indonesia (Patrinos and Ariasingam 1997). Financial incentives to families that allow their children to attend school and programs that channel public funds for education through beneficiaries and their families can be efficient and effective uses of resources. Such schemes could be important for financing lifelong learning in the developing world.

Individual Learning Accounts

Individual learning accounts (ILAs) encourage savings for education while providing vouchers to people interested in pursuing training. An ILA is a base amount of resources set aside for an individual to use for his or her learning. ILAs can be used to develop knowledge, skills, and abilities that increase their human capital. The United Kingdom introduced such accounts (although it has since abandoned the program because of fraudulent activity by training providers), and several other European countries are either piloting or considering setting them up (box 4.10).

Box 4.10. Individual Learning Accounts in Western Europe

The Netherlands: An ILA initiative has been running in the Netherlands since 2001. It involves eight pilot projects, each serving up to 150 people. The project includes contributions from learners, employers, and the state. State contributions are budgeted at about $400 per learner; employers contribute about $130–$400 per learner. So far the pilot has been confined to particular training fields.

The Netherlands intends to launch personal development accounts (PDAs) in 2003. Like ILAs, PDAs promote lifelong learning by offering a subsidy to learners using a personal account. PDAs use tax incentives for contributions made to the account. ILAs are expected to expire shortly after the PDAs are introduced.

Both employees and employers show interest in this scheme, with trainees motivated by actually managing the account. ILAs can be an effective stimulus for learners with few skills, who would not otherwise participate in additional training.

Spain: The Basque Country launched a program in September 2000 that gives secondary school teachers vouchers worth $130–$600. The funds cover 75 percent of training costs and are intended to be used for enhancing computer skills.

Sweden: Sweden has proposed creating ILAs in which learners and employers deposit funds for competency training. These funds would be tax free when placed in the account but treated as income once withdrawn. Accumulating assets in the learning account would thus allow learners to defer taxes. The subsidy comes as a tax reduction when the individual withdraws funds from the account. The tax reduction depends on two factors: the amount the individual withdraws and the "scope of competency development," measured by a predetermined scale for each kind of training. The proposal thus uses a voucher that is proportional to the amount invested by the individual and to an objective measurement of the intensity of the program.

As an alternative to state-sponsored initiatives, the corporation Scandia introduced "competency assurance" accounts in Sweden. These accounts allow learners to save up to 20 percent of their income for future use to cover training expenses and, when studying full time, forgone income. The employer contributes the same amount that the learner does to the account. This example stands out as a private initiative to financing lifelong learning.

United Kingdom: The United Kingdom introduced ILAs in 1997 to encourage learners to take responsibility for their learning. Learners received about $215 for opening an account; thereafter they obtained

(continued)

Box 4.10. (*Continued*)

discounts of 20 percent for additional training at approved learning providers (80 percent for basic computing, numeracy, and literacy courses). Contributions to an ILA by an employer were tax free, constituting an additional contribution from the state.

Government officials closed the system after receiving clear evidence of abuse and fraud. Some unscrupulous learning providers used learners' personal information to claim discounts from the government without learners' knowledge. A few providers increased their prices to take advantage of the additional demand created by the discounts offered by government.

Source: Palacios 2002.

In the United States individual development accounts (IDAs)—dedicated savings accounts similar in structure to Individual Retirement Accounts (IRAs)—can be used only for education, job training, capitalizing a small business, or purchasing a first home. The accounts are managed by community organizations and held at local financial institutions. Contributions for lower-income participants are matched using both private and public sources (Edwards 1997; Scanlon 2001). Education Savings Accounts (ESAs) in Canada use the same general approach (box 4.11). Unlike in an entitlement program, in which each learner is entitled to a certain amount, in an ESA the amount to which a person is entitled depends on the amount saved and the kind of training pursued.

Financing Lifelong Learning in Developing Countries and Transition Economies

An idea worth pursuing, especially in developing countries and transition economies, is the subsidy/loan package. This kind of program allows learners to save and invest in building their human capital, and it meets the financing needs of people at different stages in the learning cycle. A package to encourage lifelong learning through sustainable mechanisms would consider the interaction between motivation for learning and financing needs. The focus would be on motivating learners to acquire new, productive skills throughout the lifecycle. Thus subsidies would play a larger role for low-income learners, and loans (at market interest rates) would be more important for higher-income and more highly motivated groups. The idea is to facilitate and encourage the accumulation of savings and assets while increasing incentives to invest in education. The role of the government as a provider of information would become critical to ensure effective decisionmaking.

Box 4.11. Financing Lifelong Learning through Education Savings Accounts in Canada

Canada's Learn/Save program stresses the role of savings for financing lifelong learning. Under the program an individual's contributions are matched by the state in a ratio of 3 to 1. The maximum amount that an individual can save is about $3,750 a year. Program participants, or their families, can use the funds in the account for learning activities or to capitalize a small business. Learn/Save targets low-income families.

One of the interesting features of Learn/Save is the evaluation program the government plans to use to assess its effectiveness. The evaluation, which will be conducted by an independent research organization, will draw on surveys of more than 4,600 learners 18, 36, and 54 months after the initiation of the program. The study will compare the results among people who received only financial support, people who also received other kinds of support, and a control group.

Source: Palacios 2002.

Government and donor funds for financial grants and vouchers must reach the largest number of learners possible, targeting those who need help most. Since financial barriers (including forgone earnings) are one of the most important reasons people drop out of school, the size of the grant should be adjusted to the amount needed to provide learners with the motivation to participate. Simple means tests would go a long way toward reducing poorly targeted public expenditures and not crowd out private contributions (McMahon 1989). Means tests are unnecessary at basic education levels, since primary education needs to be delivered universally; they are not needed in the case of most government-guaranteed student loan schemes (since learners are expected to repay).

Attracting private capital to finance lifelong learning remains a challenge. The main barriers are the difficulty of assessing future earnings and collecting from large numbers of borrowers. None of the programs cited in this chapter has been successful in attracting private resources (except the very small MyRichUncle, which operates in a high-income country). Partial public subsidy through means-tested vouchers supplemented by financial grants to help with living costs can attract private capital. This is because private financiers acknowledge that learners, who bear part of the cost of their training, have incentive to participate in their learning activities. Furthermore, there is viable demand for the services provided.

The financing of lifelong learning requires continued public spending on levels of education where social returns exceed private returns (basic knowledge and competencies), a greater private role in investments that yield higher private returns (tertiary, continuing education), and government intervention targeting low-income individuals to achieve greater equity. Thus the financing of lifelong learning requires a menu of options that are sustainable and equitable—ideally a strategic mix of cost-sharing and voucher schemes.

Conclusion

Offering a variety of financing options may be helpful in responding to diverse needs. Governments typically use a wide variety of mechanisms to fund both learners and institutions. These programs work in different ways and create different incentives (and disincentives); interactions between them can be complex. Policymakers need to ensure alignment. The following chapter addresses the need to benchmark performance of a country's learning system within the global knowledge economy and takes up the issue of reform.

5
Moving Forward

L'éducation ne devrait pas abandonner les individus au moment où ils sortent des écoles, elle devrait embrasser tous les âges . . . assurer aux hommes dans tous les âges de la vie la facilité de conserver leurs connaissances ou d'en acquérir de nouvelles.

[Education should not end when individuals leave school, it should embrace all ages . . . to ensure that men at each stage of their lives are able to maintain their knowledge or acquire new knowledge.]

Diderot, 1792

To participate in the emerging knowledge economy, people need to update their skills continuously. Lifelong learning will thus become a norm. Providing lifelong learning entails securing affordable access to a variety of learning opportunities, both formal and nonformal. This means that the learning system and its governance must change and that more resources will have to be allocated. Given limited public resources, relying on cost-sharing, involving private providers, and increasing the efficiency of the education system are critical. Creating a lifelong learning framework based on these principles requires complex changes in a country's entire learning system.

Developing countries and transition economies are at risk of being further marginalized in a competitive global knowledge economy because their education systems are not prepared to support the acquisition and application of knowledge. This lack of preparation stems from the low coverage and low quality of education and training, outdated curricula and the lack of feedback mechanisms, the overemphasis on rote learning and exam outcomes, the lack of institutional diversification of learning providers, the inappropriate role of the state, and the lack of articulation between different aspects of the system.

Benchmarking National Systems of Lifelong Learning

One way countries could move forward would be by establishing national benchmarks for measuring lifelong learning outcomes. Such measures are underdeveloped. Traditional measures of educational progress, such as gross enrollment ratios and public spending as a proportion of GDP, do not capture important dimensions of lifelong learning. Gross enrollment ratios measure inputs rather than the achievement of core or other competencies; public spending does not include the substantial amount of private spending on training in most countries. Traditional indicators often fail to capture nonformal and informal learning, such as that which takes place in the workplace or outside the formal education and training system, activities that are becoming increasingly important.

Most developing countries will need to make many changes as they move toward a lifelong learning system in which people have access to many types of learning opportunities. It is unrealistic to embark on everything at once, however, and developing countries will need to develop realistic strategies with which to proceed. An important step is to identify the current situation, particularly with respect to systems of international peers.

Much international information is available that can help countries benchmark their performance, both in terms of inputs (unit costs of education and training, student-teacher ratio, teaching time in learning activities) and outputs (learner assessment). International assessments, such as the Third International Mathematics and Science Study (TIMSS), the International Association for Evaluation of Educational Achievement Citizenship and Education Study (CES), the Programme for International Student Assessment (PISA), the International Adult Literacy Study Survey (IALS), and the new Adult Literacy and Lifeskills Survey (ALL), can help countries identify their relative weaknesses and strengths within an internationally developed framework. In Chile, for example, poor performance on the IALS created an awareness of the need for more relevant policies and programs. These assessments focus increasingly on the key competencies for effective participation in the knowledge economy (table 5.1).

At the national level, school-level data are rarely collected and analyzed in most developing countries and transition economies. Case studies from six Central and Eastern European countries suggest that lack of

Table 5.1. Competencies Assessed by Various International Assessments

Competency	TIMSS	PISA	IALS	ALL	CES
Literacy		✓	✓	✓	
Numeracy	✓	✓	✓	✓	
Scientific literacy	✓	✓			
Problem solving		2003		✓	
Information and communication technologies		2006		✓	
Working with others				✓	✓
Tacit knowledge		✓			
Capacity to manage learning		✓			
Attitude toward learning	✓	✓			
Civics knowledge					✓

Notes: Different assessments often measure different aspects of the same competency (see chapter 2 for examples). PISA will measure competence in problem-solving in 2003 and adeptness with information and communication technologies in 2006.
Source: OECD 2001e, 2002c.

transparent, accurate, and timely information is an important barrier to improving access and quality of learning (World Bank Institute 2001b).

Countries can gauge their progress toward creating lifelong learning opportunities based on a set of indicators (table 5.2). The list is not comprehensive, and not all of the measures are applicable to all countries. More refined ways of measuring progress are needed.

The Permanent Nature of Change

Continuous reform is needed not only to accelerate the pace of reform but also to deepen the extent to which fundamental transformations of learning are carried out (New Zealand, Information Technology Advisory Group 1999). Implementation of these strategies will, however, have to take into account the political aspects of reform. The traditional model of education reform is not amenable to constant change: a stream of initiatives and policy changes becomes overwhelming to education stakeholders, and reform fatigue and resistance set in. Institutions themselves must take responsibility for their own change, evolution, and improvement in response to learner demand and institutional performance. The incentive and regulatory frameworks must encourage them to do so.

Table 5.2. Measuring a Country's Advance toward Lifelong Learning

Lifelong learning concept	Measures/indicators	Examples from developing countries or transition economies
Transformation of learning		
Identifying new skills and competencies (knowledge creation and application)	• Adoption of national standards and accreditation systems • Participation and improvement of learners • Adult performance in assessments that measure new skills	• Romania Higher Education Project, Romania Education Reform Project, Chile Lifelong Learning Project (definition of standards, accreditation, assessment mechanisms) • Participation in IALS: Chile, Czech Republic, Hungary, Poland, Slovenia • Participation in PISA: Brazil, Czech Republic, Hungary, Latvia, Mexico, Poland, Russian Federation • Participation in TIMSS: 17 developing countries in 1995, 22 developing countries in 1999
Change in learning process	• Adoption of learner-centered education practices • Alignment of quality control mechanisms (curriculum, learning materials, and assessment) to implement learner-centered pedagogy • Changes in teacher education and training focusing on learner-centered pedagogical practice	• Active learning and learner-centered pedagogy: Guatemala • Use of ICT as levers for change in the learning process: Chile, Costa Rica • Reform of secondary education: Jamaica • Teacher training for learner-centered pedagogy: Jamaica's Reform of Secondary Education

- Increase in flexible delivery of learning opportunities (for example, distance education, use of ICTs)

- Changed quality assurance mechanisms (certification and accreditation)

- Interactive radio instruction for primary education: Bolivia, Kenya, Nicaragua, South Africa, Thailand
- Distance teacher training program: Botswana, Kenya, Malawi, Swaziland, Uganda
- Joint degree programs: Singapore
- Telecenters: Benin, India, Mali, Mozambique, Pakistan, Philippines, Senegal
- National evaluation or independent accreditation agencies for higher education: Argentina, Chile, Colombia, El Salvador, Ghana, Hungary, Indonesia, Jordan, Nigeria, Romania, Slovenia

Governance

Outcome-driven governance

- Improvement in articulation between different types of learning and recognition of informal learning
- Competency-based assessment and qualification
- Policy deepening linkage between education and labor market

- New articulation system: Chile
- Competency-based national assessment: Romania, South Africa
- Skills training programs including integrating conventional literacy programs with livelihoods training programs: Hungary, Nepal, Romania, Uganda

(continued)

Table 5.2. Measuring a Country's Advance toward Lifelong Learning (*Continued*)

Lifelong learning concept	*Measures/indicators*	*Examples from developing countries or transition economies*
Enabling governance	• Increase in degree of administrative and financial decentralization and participation of stakeholders in decision-making process • Increase in degree of openness within a country and toward international community	• Increased enrollment, education coverage, and local capacity building as a result of decentralization: El Salvador, India, Nicaragua • Open investment policy for foreign direct investment: Costa Rica
Inclusive and effective governance	• Decline in inequity between and within countries through policy measures (for example, engagement of the poor, provision of information) • Adoption of sound education management system (for example, use of information in government operations, focus on outcomes) with monitoring and evaluation system	• TV-based education expanding learning opportunities of remote areas: Brazil, Mexico • Cost-effective delivery of management control using an Integrated Financial Management System (IFMS): Tanzania • E-procurement: Chile, Mexico • E-citizens initiative: Brazil, South Africa • Information boutiques: Burkina Faso
Responsive governance	• Improvement in accountability and transparency (e-government and greater participatory approaches and openness about policy intentions, formulation, and implementation) • Creation of legal regulatory framework that creates level playing field between public and private providers and provides information about institutional performance	• Implementation of diagnostic Public Expenditure Tracking Surveys (PETS): Ghana, Tanzania, Uganda • Strong legal basis to promote education and lifelong learning: Brazil (1996 Education Law) • Publication of institutional results: Chile

Financing options

Increased spending on lifelong learning	• Increase in share of total education resources	• Lifelong learning framework: Chile
Cost-sharing among stakeholders	• Use of traditional loans, human capital contracts, graduate tax, income-contingent repayment loans	• Income-contingent loans: Chile (the University Credit), Ghana, Hungary, Namibia (use of social security system for cost recovery)
Targeted subsidization to promote equity	• Use of vouchers, entitlements, individual learning accounts, education savings accounts, learning tax credits	• Vouchers: Bangladesh, Chile (indirect fiscal contribution contingent on the amount of the highest performance of first-year students enrolled), Guatemala, Pakistan
Changing roles of government	• Decrease in direct administration and increase in subsidies in certain types of learning	• Subsidy/loan package to reduce child labor: Brazil (Bolsa Escola)

Another source of anxiety for policymakers is the lack of a blueprint for change. All countries—industrial and developing countries alike—are struggling to put the pieces together to make their education and training systems more responsive to the needs of today and tomorrow. As the traditional education and training institutions come under attack for being unresponsive and their services are delivered by an array of niche providers, institutions will have to examine what type of learning institutions will emerge as valuable and valued and how policymakers should support them.

The World Bank's Support for Lifelong Learning

The theme of lifelong learning has been embraced by the OECD, the European Union, the World Bank, and other international organizations. In 1999 World Bank President James Wolfensohn referred explicitly to lifelong learning as a component of what education means for poverty alleviation (World Bank 1999d).

The World Bank has developed strategies for traditional education, but its involvement is still at an early stage and it has not yet fully explored the implications of lifelong learning. Some work has been done, however (table 5.3). *Priorities and Strategies for Education* (World Bank 1995) emphasized lifelong learning and private provision of education. Also notable was the attention to nonpublic provision in *Higher Education: The Lessons of Experience* (World Bank 1994). The regional strategy for transition economies of Europe (World Bank 2000a) was the strongest in terms of lifelong learning concepts and nonpublic provision. Cross-sectoral strategies tackle private provision (IFC 2001) and some lifelong learning concepts (for example, World Bank 2002f). Three projects with lifelong learning components have been implemented ($5.6 million in Romania, $71 million in Chile, and $150 million in Hungary) (box 5.1), and the World Bank is working with the government of Jordan to develop an e-learning strategy for the knowledge economy (box 5.2). Most of these strategies, however, have looked at individual elements of the lifelong learning system rather than seeing the overall framework and connections between these elements.

As lifelong learning becomes a priority in more and more countries, the World Bank will need to articulate a comprehensive strategy for education and the knowledge economy. That strategy will then need to be translated into concrete operations in specific countries. The World Bank will continue to work on this important question by disseminating its strategies, developing diagnostic tools, and undertaking studies on particular countries.

The themes the World Bank will address include changing learning paradigms brought about by the knowledge economy, resources for lifelong

Table 5.3. Lifelong Learning in World Bank Documents

Type	Document Title
Education sector policy papers	• Priorities and Strategies for Education (World Bank 1995) • Education Sector Strategy (World Bank 1999b) • Vocational and Technical Education and Training (World Bank 1991b) • Higher Education: The Lessons of Experience (World Bank 1994) • Constructing Knowledge Societies: New Challenges for Tertiary Education (World Bank 2002c)
Regional strategies	• Education and Training in the East Asia and Pacific Region (World Bank 1998b) • Education in the Middle East and North Africa (World Bank 1999a) • Educational Change in Latin America and the Caribbean (World Bank 1999c) • A Chance to Learn: Knowledge and Finance for Education in Sub-Saharan Africa (World Bank 2001d) • Hidden Challenges to Education Systems in Transition Economies (World Bank 2000a)
Cross-sectoral strategies	• Social Protection Sector Strategy: From Safety Net to Springboard (World Bank 2001h) • World Bank Strategy for Science and Technology in Development (World Bank 2002h) • Information and Communication Technologies (World Bank 2002f) • Rural Strategy: Reaching the Poor (World Bank 2002g) • Investing in Private Education (IFC 2001)
Projects	• Hungary: Human Resources Project (World Bank 1991a) • Romania: Reform of Higher Education and Research Project (World Bank 1996) • Chile: Lifelong Learning and Training Project (World Bank 2002b)

learning, governance and management challenges for the new learning system, and the equity aspects of lifelong learning. An assessment toolkit will measure a country's progress toward lifelong learning. Research and pilot studies, conducted in collaboration with development partners, will focus on distance learning, ICTs, knowledge and skills, lifelong learning and training policies, knowledge transfer, rural women's knowledge, capacity building, and career development and guidance. Case studies

Box 5.1. Hungary's Strategy for Lifelong Learning

A $150 million project, successfully completed in 1997, was initiated by the Hungarian government immediately after the move to a democratic market economy. The primary goals of the project were to adapt human resources institutions to emerging economic and social demand and to facilitate lifelong learning for a developing knowledge economy. The project was comprehensive and included employment and training, higher education, and research components.

The employment and training component developed career guidance and information services to promote labor mobility; improved occupational training and continuing education for adults by providing support for labor market-based training, including a regional network of Human Resource Development Centers with strong links to private and public employers; and initiated reform of secondary schooling by developing new curricula with more general education and broader training to replace the outdated and narrow curricula that had been used in vocational schools.

The higher education and research components supported the introduction of competition-based grant funding for higher education programs based on criteria that emphasized greater collaboration and resource sharing among institutions of higher education and research as well as new interdisciplinary programs. It developed a program of practically oriented foreign language training. It also supported the development of human resources for science and technology by earmarking a portion of the competition-based National Scientific Research Fund (OTKA) for younger researchers, improving the management of and refurbishing the centers of scientific instrumentation financed by OTKA, and upgrading the national research and development computer network used by academic and industrial researchers.

Source: World Bank 1991a, 1998c.

Box 5.2. Developing an Education Strategy for the Knowledge Economy in Jordan

Under the leadership of King Abdullah, Jordan is establishing a national education and training strategy to help Jordan compete in the global economy. The E-Learning Strategic Framework is a comprehensive strategy for incorporating ICT in the learning process. More work is required to increase affordable access to lifelong learning opportunities, discussed during the Vision Forum held in Amman in September 2002.

will cover evaluation of possible mechanisms for financing lifelong learning, cost-effectiveness of different models of learning, teacher policies, multinational corporations and education, assessment of soft skills, indicators of lifelong learning, spending on lifelong learning, returns to lifelong learning, lifelong learning as a strategic economic strategy, and analysis of the PISA and TIMSS.

There is a need to engage national policymakers and stakeholders worldwide in a dialogue on lifelong learning, helping governments formulate visions and concrete action plans for establishing both lifelong learning and innovation frameworks appropriate to their country contexts. The World Bank can assist in this effort by helping deepen the understanding of the implications of the knowledge economy for education and training systems and by disseminating analytic documents on education for the knowledge economy.

References

Acemoglu, D., and J. Angrist. 1999. "How Large Are the Social Returns to Education? Evidence from Compulsory Schooling Laws." NBER Working Paper 7444. National Bureau of Economic Research, Cambridge, Mass.

Adey, P., and M. Shayer. 1994. "Improving Learning through Cognitive Intervention." General Teaching Council for England, London (www.gtce.org.uk/research/raisestudy.asp)

Aitken, B., A. Harrison, and R.E. Lipsey. 1996. "Wages and Foreign Ownership: A Comparative Study of Mexico, Venezuela, and the United States." *Journal of International Economics* 40 (1/2): 345–371.

Alvarez, Maria Ines, Francisca Roman, Maria Cecilia Dobles, Jeanina Umana, Magaly Zuniga, Jackeline Garcia, Barbara Means, Michael Potashnik, and Laura Rawlings. 1998. "Computers in Schools: A Qualitative Study of Chile and Costa Rica." Education and Technology Series Special Issue. World Bank, Human Development Network, Education Group, Washington, D.C.

Andrews, Les. 1997. "The Effect of HECS on Interest in Undertaking Higher Education." Department of Employment, Education, Training, and Youth Affairs, Higher Education Division, Canberra, Australia.

Angrist, Joshua, Eric Bettinger, Erik Bloom, Elizabeth King, and Michael Kremer. 2001. "Vouchers for Private Schooling in Colombia: Evidence from a Randomized Natural Experiment." NBER Working Paper 8343. National Bureau of Economic Research, Cambridge, Mass.

Anthony, Susanne. 2002. "The Voucher System: The Danish State Education Grant and Loan Scheme for Higher Education." Government of Denmark, Copenhagen. Processed.

Appiah, Elizabeth, and Walter McMahon. 2002. "The Social Outcomes of Education and Feedbacks on Growth in Africa." *Journal of Development Studies* 38 (4): 27–68.

Appleton, Simon. 2000. "Education and Health at the Household Level in Sub-Saharan Africa." Center for International Development Working Paper 33. Harvard University, Cambridge, Mass.

Appleton, Simon, and A. Balihuta. 1996. "Education and Agricultural Productivity in Uganda." *Journal of International Development* 8 (3): 415–444.

Araneda, Hernán, and Cristóbal Marín. 2002. "Meeting the Challenge of the Knowledge Economy." World Bank, Human Development Network, Education Group, Washington, D.C. Processed.

Ashton, David N. n.d. "E-Learning: Has the Bubble Burst and Just What Is it Good for?" Univeristy of Leicester, Centre for Labour Market Studies, United Kingdom. (www.clms.le.ac.uk)

Australia, Department of Education, Employment and Training (DEET). 2001. Interviewed by Cecile Fruman. Face-to-face interview. August 25, Victoria.

Autor, D.H., F. Levy, and R.J. Murnane. 2002. "Upstairs, Downstairs: Computers and Skills on Two Floors of a Large Bank." *Industrial and Labor Relations Review* 55 (3): 432–447.

Azariadis, C., and A. Drazen. 1990. "Threshold Externalities in Economic Development." *Quarterly Journal of Economics* 105 (2): 501–526.

Bakia, Marianne. 2000. "The Costs of Computers in Classrooms: Data from Developing Countries." Consortium for School Networking, Washington, D.C.

Barr, Nicholas. 2001. *The Welfare State as Piggy Bank: Information, Risk, Uncertainty, and the Role of the State.* Oxford: Oxford University Press.

Barro, Robert J. 1991. "Economic Growth in a Cross-Section of Countries." *Quarterly Journal of Economics* 106 (2):407–444.

_____. 2001 "Human Capital and Growth." *American Economic Review, Papers and Proceedings* 91 (2): 12–17.

Barro, Robert J., and Jong-Wha Lee. 2000. "International Data on Educational Attainment: Updates and Implications." Center for International Development Working Paper 42. Harvard University, Cambridge, Mass. (http://www2.cid.harvard.edu/ciddata/)

Bartel, A.P., and F.R. Lichtenberg. 1987. "The Comparative Advantage of Educated Workers in Implementing New Technology." *Review of Economics and Statistics* 69 (1): 1–11.

_____. 1988. "Technical Change, Learning, and Wages." NBER Working Paper 2732. National Bureau of Economic Research, Cambridge, Mass.

Bedi, Arjun S., and Andrzej Cieoelik. 2002. "Wages and Wage Growth in Poland: The Role of Foreign Direct Investment." *Economics of Transition* 10 (1): 1–27.

Benhabib, J., and M.M. Spiegel. 1994. "Role of Human Capital in Economic Development: Evidence from Aggregate Cross-Country Data." *Journal of Monetary Economics* 34: 143–173.

Berman, E., and S. Machin. 2000. "Skill-Biased Technology Transfer around the World." *Oxford Review of Economic Policy* 16 (3): 12–22.

Blom, Andreas, Lauritz Holm-Nielsen, and Dorte Verner. 2001. "Education, Earnings, and Inequality in Brazil, 1982–98: Implications for Education Policy." World Bank, Latin America and the Caribbean Region, Education Sector Unit, Washington, D.C.

Blomström, Magnus, and Ari Kokko. 2001. "From Natural Resources to High-Tech Production: The Evolution of Industrial Competitiveness in Sweden and Finland." Stockholm School of Economics, Sweden.

Botelho, Caren Addis, and Lara Goldmark. 2000. "Paraguay Vouchers Revisited: Strategies for the Development of Training Markets." Paper presented at conference on Business Services for Small Enterprises in Asia: Developing Markets and Measuring Performance, Hanoi, April 3–6. (www.ilo.org/public/english/employment/ent/papers/voucher.htm)

Bransford, John D., Ann L. Brown, and Rodney R. Cocking, eds. 2000. *How People Learn: Brain, Mind, Experience, and School.* Expanded ed. Washington, D.C.: National Academy Press.

Bray, Mark. 2000. *Double-Shift Schooling: Design and Operation for Cost-Effectiveness.* London: Commonwealth Secretariat and United Nations Educational, Scientific, and Cultural Organization (UNESCO) International Institute for Educational Planning (IIEP).

Bregman, A., and A. Marom. 1993. "Growth Factors in Israel's Business Sector, 1958–1988." Discussion Paper 93.02. Bank of Israel Research Department, Jerusalem.

Brown, P., and H. Lauder. 2000. "The Future of Skill Formation in Singapore." Working Paper 3. Cardiff University, School of Social Sciences, United Kingdom.

Camhi, Rosita, and Rosana Latuf. 2000. "Evaluación del Sistema de Ayudas Estudiantiles a la Educación Superior." Working paper. Instituto Libertad y Desarrollo, Santiago, Chile.

Capper, Joanne. 2000. "Teacher Training and Technology: An Overview of Case Studies and Lessons Learned." *Techknowlogia* 2 (6) (November/December): 17–19.

Carlson, Beverley A. 2001. "Education and the Labour Market in Latin America: Why Measurement Is Important and What it Tells Us about Policies, Reforms, and Performance." Desarrollo Productivo Serie 114. Economic Commission for Latin America and Caribbean (CEPAL), Santiago, Chile.

Castro-Leal, Florencia, Julia Dayton, Lionel Demery, and Kalpana Mehra. 1999. "Public Social Spending in Africa: Do the Poor Benefit?" *World Bank Research Observer* 14 (1): 49–72.

Cawthera, Andy. 2001. "Computers in Secondary Schools in Developing Countries: Costs and Other Issues." DFID Education Research Paper 43. London: Department for International Development.

Chapman, Bruce. 2001. "The Australian Income Contingent Charge for Higher Education: Lessons from the Colonies." Paper presented at the Funding Higher Education in the 21st Century Conference, University of Nottingham, United Kingdom, November 5.

Cibulka, James, Sharon Coursey, Michelle Nakayama, Jeremy Price, and Shelly Stewart. 2000. "Schools as Learning Organizations: A Review of the Literature." University of Maryland, National Partnership for Excellence and Accountability in Teaching, College Park. (www.ericsp.org/pages/digests/ProfDevLitRev.htm)

Craig, Helen J., Richard J. Kraft, and Joy du Plessis. 1998. "Teacher Development: Making an Impact." USAID and World Bank, Washington, D.C.

Dar, Amit, and Indermit S. Gill. 1998. "Evaluating Retraining Programs in OECD Countries: Lessons Learned." *World Bank Research Observer* 13 (1): 79–101.

Davis, Stan, and Christopher Meyer. 2000. *Future Wealth*. Boston, Mass.: Harvard Business School Press.

De Baessa, Yetilú, Ray Chesterfield, and Tanya Ramos. 2002 "Active Learning and Democratic Behaviour in Guatemalan Rural Primary Schools." *Compare* 32 (2): 205–218.

Delannoy, Françoise. 2000. "Education Reforms in Chile, 1980–98: A Lesson in Pragmatism." Country Studies, Education Reforms and Management Publication Series 1 (1). World Bank, Human Development Network, Education Group, Washington, D.C.

Desforges, Charles. 2000. "Familiar Challenges and New Approaches: Necessary Advance in Theory and Methods in Research on Teaching and Learning." Desmond Nuttall/Carfax Memorial Lecture, British Educational Research Association Conference, Cardiff, United Kingdom, September 7–9.

_____. 2001. "Knowledge Base for Teaching and Learning." *Teaching and Learning Research Programme Newsletter* 3: 3–4.

Dohmen, Dieter. 2000. "Vouchers in Higher Education: A Practical Approach." Paper presented at the Education and Socio-Economical Research & Consulting (ECER) Conference, Cologne, Germany, September 20–23.

Edwards, Karen. 1997. "Individual Development Accounts: Creative Savings for Families and Communities." Working paper. University of Washington, Center for Social Development, St. Louis.

European Industrial Relations Observatory Online. March 1999. "Comparative on Work Organisation: The Netherlands." (www.eiro.eurofound.ie/1999/03/word/nl9903123s.doc)

Farrell, Glen M., ed. 2001. *The Changing Faces of Virtual Education*. Vancouver: Commonwealth of Learning.

Feenstra, R.C., D. Madani, T.-H. Yang, and C.-Y. Liang. 1999. "Testing Endogenous Growth in South Korea and Taiwan." *Journal of Development Economics* 60 (2): 317–341.

Fiske, Edward. 1996. *Decentralization of Education: Politics and Consensus*. Washington, D.C.: World Bank.

Fretwell, David, and Joe Colombano. 2000. "Adult Continuing Education: An Integral Part of Lifelong Learning: Emerging Policies and Programs for the 21st Century in Upper- and Middle-Income Countries." Human Development Network Working Paper 22062. World Bank, Washington, D.C.

Fretwell, David, Morgan V. Lewis, and Arjen Deij. 2001. "A Framework for Defining and Assessing Occupational and Training Standards in Developing Countries." ERIC Clearinghouse on Adult, Career, and Vocational Education, Columbus, Ohio, World Bank, Washington, D.C., and European Training Foundation, Turin, Italy.

Friedman, Milton. 1955. "The Role of Government in Education." In Robert A. Solo, ed., *Economics and the Public Interest*. New Brunswick, New Jersey: Rutgers University Press.

Friedman, Milton, and Simon Kuznets. 1945. *Income from Independent Professional Practice*. New York: National Bureau of Economic Research.

Fuchs, V., and D.M. Reklis. 1994. "Mathematical Achievement in Eighth Grade: Interstate and Racial Differences." NBER Working Paper 4784. National Bureau of Economic Research, Cambridge, Mass.

Georgiades, Kyriakos A. 2001. "Use of Technology in World Bank Education Projects: An Operational Review, Fiscal Years 1997–2000." World Bank, Human Development Network, Washington, D.C. Processed.

Gerster, Richard, ed. 2001. "Linking Work, Skills, and Knowledge: Learning or Survival and Growth." Swiss Agency for Development and Cooperation (SDC), Berne. (http://www.workandskills.ch/downloads/ConferenceReportWS.pdf)

Gill, Indermit S., Fred Fluitman, and Amit Dar. 2000. *Vocational Education and Training Reform: Matching Skills to Markets and Budgets*. New York: Oxford University Press.

Göbel, K., and H.-G. Hesse. Forthcoming. "A Measurement Device for the Assessment of Intercultural Competence in the English as a Foreign Language Class." Frankfurt: Deutsches Institut für Internationale Pädagogische Forschung (DIPF).

Grace, Jeremy, Charles Kenny, Christine Qiang, Jia Liu, and Taylor Reynolds. 2001. "Information and Communication Technologies and Broad-Based Development: A Partial Review of the Evidence."

Greenough, W. 2000. "Brain's Mechanisms of Learning and Memory." Paper presented at the First High-Level Forum on Learning Sciences and Brain Research: Potential Implications for Education Policies and Practices: Brain Mechanisms and Early Learning, Sackler Institute, New York, June 16–17, organized by the OECD. (www.oecd.org/pdf/M00019000/M00019809.pdf)

Gundlach, E. 2001. "Education and Economic Development: An Empirical Perspective." *Journal of Economic Development* 26 (1): 37–60.

Haan, Hans C., with Nicholas Serriere. 2002. *Training for Work in the Informal Sector: Fresh Evidence from West and Central Africa.* Turin: International Training Centre of the International Labor Office.

Hammer, M.R., and M.J. Bennett. 1998. *The Intercultural Development Inventory Manual.* Portland, Ore.: Intercultural Communication Institute.

Hanushek, Eric A., and Dennis D. Kimko. 2000. "Schooling, Labor-Force Quality, and the Growth of Nations." *American Economic Review* 90 (5): 1184–1208.

Heckman, James, and P.J. Klenow. 1997. "Human Capital Policy." University of Chicago, Department of Economics, Chicago, Ill.

Heckman, James J., Rebecca L. Roselius, and Jeffrey A. Smith. 1994. "U.S. Education and Training Policy: A Reevaluation of the Underlying Assumptions behind the 'New Consensus.'" In A. Levenson and L.C. Solmon, eds., *Labor Markets, Employment Policy, and Job Creation.* Santa Monica, Calif.: Milken Institute.

Heeks, Richard. 2001. "Understanding E-Governance for Development." I-Government Working Paper 11. University of Manchester, Institute for Development Policy and Management, United Kingdom. (http://idpm.man.ac.uk/idpm/igov11.htm)

Hepp, Pedro K., S. Enrique Hinostroza, M. Ernesto Laval, and F. Lucio Rebién. Forthcoming. "Technology in Schools: Advice for Policymakers." World Bank, Washington, D.C.

Hong, W. Tan, and Geeta Batra. 1995. "Enterprise Training in Five Developing Countries: Overview of Incidence, Determinants, and Productivity Outcomes." Paper presented at the Conference on Enterprise Training Strategies and Productivity, World Bank, Washington, D.C., June 12–13.

Houle, C.O. 1961. *The Inquiring Mind: A Study of the Adult Who Continues to Learn.* Madison: University of Wisconsin Press.

Howie, S. J., T.A. Marsh, J. Allummoottil, M. Glencross, C. Deliwe, and C.A. Hughes. 2000. "Middle School Students' Performance in Mathematics in the Third International Mathematics and Science Study: South African Realities." *Studies in Educational Evaluation* 26 (1): 61–77.

Huffman, Jane B., and Kristine A. Hipp. 2001. "Creating Communities of Learners: The Interaction of Shared Leadership, Shared Vision, and Supportive Conditions." *International Journal of Education Reform* 10 (3): 215–235.

IFC (International Finance Corporation). 2001. *Investing in Private Education: IFC's Strategic Directions.* Washington, D.C.

Japan, Ministry of Education, Science, Sports and Culture (MESSC). 1991. "Japanese Government Policies in Education, Science and Culture 1991." In White Paper Database. Tokyo.

Jeria, Ana Maria, and Kate Hovde. 2002. "Education for All Case Study: Expansion of Secondary Education for Girls." World Bank, Human Development Network, Education Group, Washington, D.C.

Johanson, Richard K., and Arvil V. Adams. 2003. "Skills Development in Sub-Saharan Africa." World Bank, Africa Region, Human Development Network, Washington D.C.

Johnstone, Bruce. 2001. "The Economics and Politics of Income-Contingent Repayment Plans." State University of New York, Buffalo. (www.gse.buffalo.edu/FAS/Johnston/Loans.html)

Johnstone, D. Bruce, and Abebayehu Aemero. 2001. "The Applicability for Developing Countries of Income-Contingent Loans or Graduate Taxes, with Special Consideration of an Australian HECS-Type Income-Contingent Loan Program for Ethiopia." State University of New York, Graduate School of Education, Buffalo, New York. (www.gse.buffalo.edu/org/IntHigherEdFinance/textForSite/ApptoDevCountry.pdf)

Kaplan, Leslie S., and William A. Owings. 2001. "Teacher Quality and Student Achievement: Recommendations for Principals." *National Association of Secondary School Principals Bulletin* 85 (628) (November). (www.principals.org/news/bltn_tch_qul_stdnt_ach1101.html)

Kartovaara, Eija. 1996. "Secondary Education in Finland." Council of Europe, Strasbourg, France.

Kettle, Donald F. 1999. "Global Reinvention: Basic Issues, Questions Ahead." Paper prepared for the Global Forum on Reinventing Government, U.S. Department of State, Washington, D.C., Jan. 14–15. (www.brook.edu/dybdocroot/Views/Papers/Kettl/global.htm)

Klaus, David, Charlie Tesar, and Jane Shore. 2002. "Language of Instruction: A Critical Factor in Achieving Education for All." World Bank, Human Development Network, Education Group, Washington, D.C. Processed.

Klazar, Stanislav, Milan Sedmihradsky, and Alena Vancurova. 2001. "Returns of Education in the Czech Republic." *International Tax and Public Finance* 8 (4): 609–620.

Klor de Alva, Jorge. 2001. "Beyond U.S. Borders: Analyzing Investment Potential in International Markets." Paper presented at the Education Industry Investment Forum, Phoenix, Arizona, March 13.

Koda, Yoshiko. 2002. "Benchmarking to International Assessments: Diagnosing Education System Towards the Knowledge Economy." World Bank, Human Development Network, Education Group, Washington, D.C. Processed.

Krueger, Alan B., and Mikael Lindahl. 1999. "Education for Growth in Sweden and the World." NBER Working Paper 7190. National Bureau of Economic Research, Cambridge, Mass.

Larsen, Kurt, Rosemary Morris, and John P. Martin. 2001. "Trade in Educational Services: Trends and Emerging Issues." Working Paper CERI/CD/RD (2001) 6. OECD, Paris.

Leithwood, Kenneth A., Karen Edge, and Doris Jantzi. 1999. *Educational Accountability: The State of the Art*. Gütersloh: Bertelsmann Foundation Publishers.

Levin, Henry M. 2002. "Post-Compulsory Entitlements: Vouchers for Life-Long Learning." Occasional Paper 46. Columbia University, Teachers College, National Center for the Study of Privatization in Education, New York.

Levin, Henry M., and Hans G. Schütze, eds. 1983. *Financing Recurrent Education*. Beverly Hills, Calif.: Sage Publications.

Lewin, Keith, and Françoise Caillods. 2001. *Financing Secondary Education in Developing Countries: Strategies for Sustainable Growth*. Paris: United Nations Educational, Scientific, and Cultural Organization (UNESCO).

Li, Guo, Diane Steele, and Paul Glewwe. 1999. "Distribution of Government Education Expenditures in Developing Countries: Preliminary Estimates." World Bank, Development Research Group, Poverty Team, Washington, D.C.

Linden, Toby. 2001. "Double-Shift Secondary Schools: Possibilities and Issues." Secondary Education Series. World Bank, Human Development Network, Education Group, Washington, D.C.

Lizardi, Anthony. 2002. "Virtual High Schools: Development, Trends, and Issues." *Techknowlogia* 42 (2) (April–June): 36–39.

Lucas, R.E. 1988. "On the Mechanics of Economic Development." *Journal of Monetary Economics* 22 (1): 3–22.

Maman, Carole, and Tanya Scobie. 2002. "Burkina Faso: Public-Private Partnership in Education Initiative under Post-Primary Education Project." International Finance Corporation, Health and Education Department, Washington, D.C.

Mandinach, Ellen B., and Hugh F. Cline. 1994. *Classroom Dynamics: Implementing a Technology-Based Learning Environment*. Hillsdale, N.J.: Lawrence Erlbaum.

Mankiw, N. Gregory, David Romer, and David Weil. 1992. "A Contribution to the Empirics of Economic Growth." *Quarterly Journal of Economics* 107 (2): 407–437.

Martin, Michael O., Ina V.S. Mullis, Eugenio J. Gonzalez, Kelvin D. Gregory, Teresa A. Smith, Steven J. Chrostowski, Robert A. Garden, and Kathleen M. O'Connor. 2000. *TIMSS 1999 International Science Report: Findings from IEA's Repeat of the Third International Mathematics and Science Study at the Eighth Grade.* Chestnut Hill, Mass.: Boston College, Lynch School of Education, International Study Center.

McMahon, Walter W. 1989. "Potential Resource Recovery in Higher Education in the Developing Countries and the Parents' Expected Contribution." *Economics of Education Review* 7 (1): 135–52.

Merriam, Sharan B. 1993. "Adult Learning: Where Have We Come From? Where Are We Headed?" In Sharan B. Merriam, ed., *An Update on Adult Learning Theory.* San Francisco: Jossey-Bass.

____. 2001. *The New Update on Adult Learning Theory: New Directions for Adult and Continuing Education.* San Francisco: Jossey-Bass.

Middleton, John, Adrian Ziderman, and Arvil Van Adams. 1993. *Skills for Productivity: Vocational Education and Training in Developing Countries.* New York: Oxford University Press.

Mioduser, David, and Rafi Nachmias. 2002. "WWW in Education: An Overview." In H. Adelsberger, B. Colis, and M. Pawlowski, eds., *Handbook on Information Technologies and Education and Training.* New York: Springer.

Moe, Michael T., Kathleen Bailey, and Rhoda Lau. 1999. *The Book of Knowledge: Investing in the Growing Education and Training Industry.* San Francisco: Merrill Lynch and Co., Global Securities Research and Economic Group, and Global Fundamental Equity Research Department.

Mullis, Ina V.S., Michael O. Martin, Eugenio J. Gonzalez, Kelvin D. Gregory, Robert A. Garden, Kathleen M. O'Connor, Steven J. Chrostowski, and Teresa A. Smith. 2000. *TIMSS 1999 International Mathematics Report: Findings from IEA's Repeat of the Third International Mathematics and Science Study at the Eighth Grade.* Chestnut Hill, Mass.: Boston College, Lynch School of Education, International Study Center.

Murnane, Richard J., Nancy Sharkey, and Frank Levy. 2002. "Can the Internet Help Solve America's Education Problems? Lessons from the Cisco Networking Academies." In P. Grahma and N. Stacey, eds., *The Knowledge Economy and Post-Secondary Education.* Washington, D.C.: National Academy Press.

Murphy, K., and F. Welch. 1991. "The Role of International Trade in Wage Differentials." In Marvin Kosters, ed., *Workers and Their Wages: Changing Patterns in the United States.* Washington, D.C.: American Enterprise Institute.

Murray, T.S., I.S. Kirsch, and L. Jenkins. 1998. *Adult Literacy in OECD Countries: Technical Report on the First International Adult Literacy Survey.* Washington, D.C.: U.S. Department of Education, National Center for Education Statistics.

Mustard, J. Fraser. 2002. "Early Child Development and the Brain: The Base for Health, Learning, and Behavior throughout Life." In Mary Eming Young, ed., *From Early Childhood to Human Development: Investing in Our Children's Future.* Washington, D.C.: World Bank.

Muth, Rod, and Nadyne Guzman. 2000. "Learning in a Virtual Lab: Distance Education and Computer Simulations." University of Colorado, Colorado Springs, Colo. (http://web.uccs.edu/bgaddis/leadership/topicfocus3D1.htm)

Navarro, Juan Carlos, and Aimee Verdisco. 2000. *Teaching Training in Latin America: Innovations and Trends.* Washington, D.C.: Inter-American Development Bank.

Nelson, R.R., and E.S. Phelps. 1966. "Investment in Humans, Technological Diffusion, and Economic Growth." *American Economic Review* 65 (2): 69–75.

Newman, Frank, and Lara K Couturier. 2002. "Trading Public Good in the Higher Education Market." Observatory on Borderless Higher Education, London.

New Zealand, Information Technology Advisory Group to the Minister for Information Technology. 1999. *The Knowledge Economy.* Wellington, New Zealand: Ernst & Young.

Nicholls, Jane. 1998. "Student Financing in the Developing World: Applying Income-Contingent Approaches to Cost Recovery." University of Melbourne, Department of Science & Maths Education, Australia.

Nielsen, Helena Skyt, and Michael Rosholm. 2002. "Evaluation of Training in African Enterprise." World Bank, Africa Region, Human Development Department, Washington, D.C.

O'Connell, Philip J. 1999. "Adults in Training: An International Comparison of Continuing Education and Training." CERI/WD (99) 1. OECD, Paris.

O'Donoghue, Patrick J. 1998. "Fe y Alegría Starts Innovative Educational Project Amid Protests from Teachers Unions." (vheadline.com) (August 28)

OECD (Organisation for Economic Co-operation and Development). n.d. *The Financing of Lifelong Learning: Finland's Country Report for the OECD.* Paris.

____. 1992. *Education at a Glance.* Paris.

____. 1996. *Education and Training: Learning and Working in a Society in Flux.* Paris.

____. 1998a. *Education at a Glance OECD Indicators 1998.* Paris.

____. 1998b. *Staying Ahead: In-Service Training and Professional Development.* Paris.

____. 1999. "Alternative Approaches to Financing Lifelong Learning: Country Report—Denmark." Paris.

____. 2000a. *Education at a Glance 2000*. Paris.

____. 2000b. "Follow-Up of the Thematic Review on Transition from Initial Education to Working Life: Policies for Information, Guidance and Counselling Services: Making Lifelong Learning a Reality." Paris. (www.oecd.org/els/education/reviews)

____. 2000c. *Transition from Initial Education to Working Life*. Paris.

____. 2000d. *Where Are the Resources for Lifelong Learning?* Paris.

____. 2001a. *Economics and Financing of Lifelong Learning*. Paris.

____. 2001b. *Education at a Glance*. Paris.

____. 2001c. *Education Policy Analysis*. Paris.

____. 2001d. *Government of the Future*. Paris.

____. 2001e. *Knowledge and Skills for Life: First Results from PISA 2000*. Executive Summary. (www.pisa.oecd.org.)

____. 2001f. *OECD Science, Technology, and Industry Scoreboard: Towards a Knowledge-Based Economy*. Paris.

____. 2001g. "Preliminary Synthesis of the Third High Level Forum on Learning and Sciences and Brain Research: Potential Implications for Education Policies and Practices. Brain Mechanisms and Youth Learning." http://www.oecd.org/pdf/M00019000/M00019809.pdf

____. 2001h. *Thematic Review on Adult Learning: Finland Background Report*. Paris.

____. 2002a. "Definition and Selection of Competencies: Theoretical and Conceptual Foundations (DeSeCo): Strategy Paper on Key Competencies, A Frame of Reference for a Coherent Assessment and Research Program." DEELSA/ED/CERI/CD(2002)9. Paris.

____. 2002b. "ICT: Policy Challenges for Education. A Proposal." Paris.

____. 2002c. "The Role of National Qualification Systems in Promoting Lifelong Learning: Thematic Issues Groups." OECD Secretariat, Paris.

OECD and Statistics Canada 1997. *Literacy Skills for the Knowledge Society: Further Results from the International Adult Literacy Survey*. Paris.

____. 2002. *Literacy in the Information Age: Final Report of the International Adult Literacy Survey*. Paris. (www.oecd.org/EN/document/0,,EN-document-601-5-no-27-21891-601,00.html)

Oosterbeek, Hessel. 1998. "Innovative Ways to Finance Education and Their Relation to Lifelong Learning." *Education Economics* 6 (3): 219–251.

Osborn A.F., and J.E. Milbank. 1987. *The Effects of Early Education: A Report from the Child Health and Education Study*. Oxford: Clarendon Press.

Oxenham, John, Abdoul Hamid Diallo, Anne Ruhweza Katahoire, Anna Petkova-Mwangi, and Ouma Sall. 2002. "Skills and Literacy Training for Better Livelihoods: A Review of Approaches and Experiences." World Bank, Africa Region Human Development Working Paper Series. Washington, D.C.

Palacios, Miguel. 2002. "Options for Financing Lifelong Learning." World Bank, Human Development Department, Education Group, Washington, D.C. Processed.

Patrinos, Harry Anthony. 2000. "Market Forces in Education." *European Journal of Education* 35 (1): 61–79.

_____. 2001a. "The Impact of Technology on Education Premiums." World Bank, Human Development Department, Education Group, Washington, D.C. Processed.

_____. 2001b. "School Choice in Denmark." World Bank, Human Development Department, Education Group, Washington, D.C. Processed.

Patrinos, Harry Anthony, and David Lakshmanan Ariasingam. 1997. *Decentralization of Education: Demand Side Financing*. Washington, D.C.: World Bank.

Perraton, Hilary. 2000. *Open and Distance Learning in the Developing World*. London: Routledge.

Peterson, J.M. 1989. "Remediation Is No Remedy." *Educational Leadership* 46 (6): 24–25.

Pissarides, Christopher A. 2000. "Human Capital and Growth: A Synthesis Report." Technical Paper 168. OECD Development Centre, Paris.

Pohjola, M. 2000. "Information Technology and Economic Growth: A Cross-Country Analysis." World Institute for Development Economics Research Working Paper 173. United Nations University, Helsinki.

Pritchett, L. 2001. "Where Has All the Education Gone?" *World Bank Economic Review* 15 (3): 367–391.

Psacharopoulos, George. 1989. "Time Trends of the Returns to Education: Cross-National Evidence." *Economics of Education Review* 8 (3): 225–231.

Psacharopoulos, George, and Harry Anthony Patrinos. 2002. "Returns to Investment in Education: A Further Update." Policy Research Working Paper 2881. World Bank, Washington, D.C.

Putnam, Robert. 2001. "Social Capital: Measurement and Consequences." In John Helliwell, ed. *The Contribution of Human and Social Capital to Sustained Economic Growth and Well-Being*. Quebec: OECD and Human Resources.

Randriamiharisoa, Dephin. 2001. "Formal and Non-Formal Delivery of Training for Rural Producers in Madagascar." In Richard Gerster, ed., "Linking Work, Skills, and Knowledge: Learning for Survival and Growth." Swiss Agency for Development and Cooperation (SDC), Berne. (http://www.workandskills.ch/downloads/Conference ReportWS.pdf)

Rauch, J. 1993. "Productivity Gains from Geographic Concentration of Human Capital: Evidence from the Cities." *Journal of Urban Economics* 34 (3): 3–33.

Reinikka, Ritva, and Jacob Svensson. 2002. "Assessing Frontline Service Delivery." World Bank, Development Research Group, Washington, D.C.

Robbins, D.J. 1996. "Evidence on Trade and Wages in the Developing World." Technical Paper 119 (December). Paris: OECD Development Centre.

Romer, Paul M. 1989. "Human Capital and Growth: Theory and Evidence." NBER Working Paper 3173. National Bureau of Economic Research, Cambridge, Mass.

Roschelle, Jeremy M., Roy D. Pea, Christopher M. Hoadley, Douglas N. Gordin, and Barbara M. Means. 2000. "Changing How and What Children Learn in Schools with Computer-Based Technologies." *Children and Computer Technology in the Future of Children* 10 (2): 76–101. (www.futureofchildren.org/usr_doc/vol10no2Art4%2Epdf)

Rychen, Dominique Simone, and Laura Hersh Salganik, eds. 2001. *Defining and Selecting Key Competencies.* Kirkland, WA: Hogrefe and Huber.

Ryscavage, P., and P. Henle. 1990. "Earnings Inequality Accelerates in the 1980s." *Monthly Labor Review* 113 (12) (December): 3–16.

Sab, R., and S.C. Smith. 2001. "Human Capital Convergence: International Evidence." International Monetary Fund Working Paper WP/01/32. Washington, D.C.

Saint, William. 2000. "Tertiary Distance Education and Technology in Sub-Saharan Africa." Education and Technology Technical Notes Series. World Bank, Human Development Network, Education Group, Washington, D.C.

Sakellariou, C.N. 2001. "Identifying the External Effects of Human Capital: A Two-Stage Approach." *Applied Economics Letters* 8 (3): 191–194.

Scanlon, Edward. 2001. "Toward a Theory of Financial Savings and Child Well-Being: Implications for Research on a Children and Youth Savings Account Policy Demonstration." Research Background Paper CYSAPD 01–11. University of Washington, Center for Social Development, St. Louis.

Schank, Roger. 2001. "Educational Technology: The Promise and the Myth." World Bank, Human Development Network, Education Group, Washington, D.C. Processed

Scheerens, J. 1999. "School Effectiveness in Developed and Developing Countries: A Review of the Research Evidence." World Bank, Human Development Network, Education Group, Washington, D.C. Processed.

Schultz, T.W. 1975. "The Value of the Ability to Deal with Disequilibria." *Journal of Economic Literature* 13 (3): 827–846.

Sharpe, Leslie, and S. Gopinathan. 2001. "After Effectiveness: New Directions in the Singapore School System." Paper presented at the International Forum on Education Reforms in the Asia-Pacific Region: Globalization, Localization, and Individualization, Hong Kong, February 14–16.

Slaughter, M.J., and P. Swagel. 1997. "The Effect of Globalization on Wages in the Advanced Economies." International Monetary Fund Working Paper WP/97/43. Washington, D.C.

South Africa, Departments of Education and Labour. 2002. *Report of the Study Team on the Implementation of the National Qualifications Framework*. Pretoria. (www.labour.gov.za/docs/reports/NQFSTUDY.PDF)

Souza, Paulo Renato. 2002. "Post-Secondary Education and Opportunities for Investment and Trade." Paper presented at the OECD Forum on Trade in Educational Services, Washington, D.C., May 23–24. (www.oecd.org/pdf/M00030000/M00030829.pdf)

Strange, Susan. 1996. *The Retreat of the State: The Diffusion of Power in the World Economy*. New York: Cambridge University Press.

Tan, Hong W. 2000. "Information Technology and Skills in Malaysia." World Bank Institute, Washington, D.C.

Tan, Hong W., and Geeta Batra. 1995. "Enterprise Training in Developing Countries: Overview of Incidence, Determinants, and Productivity Outcomes." Private Sector Development Department Occasional Paper No. 9. World Bank, Washington, D.C.

Tatto, Maria Teresa, H. Dean Nielsen, and William K. Cummings. 1991. *Comparing the Effects and Costs of Different Approaches for Educating Primary School Teachers: The Case of Sri Lanka*. Cambridge, Mass.: Basic Research and Implementation in Developing Education Systems.

Tinbergen, J. 1975. *Income Distribution: Analysis and Policies*. Amsterdam: North-Holland.

Tooley, James N. 1999. *The Global Education Industry: Lessons from Private Education in Developing Countries*. Washington, D.C.: International Finance Corporation.

Toomey, Ron, with Christine EkinSmyth, Colin Warner, and Darrell Fraser. 2000. "A Case Study of ICT and School Improvement at Glen Waverly Secondary College, Victoria, Australia." OECD/CERI ICT Program, ICT and the Quality of Learning. (www.gwsc.vic.edu.au/oecd/oecdgwsc.pdf)

Topel, R. 1999. "Labor Markets and Economic Growth." In O. Ashenfelter and D. Card, eds., *Handbook of Labor Economics*. Vol. 3. Amsterdam: Elsevier.

Torney-Purta, Judith, R. Lehmann, H. Oswald, and W. Schulz. 2001. *Citizenship and Education in Twenty-Eight Countries: Civic Knowledge and Engagement at Age Fourteen*. Amsterdam: International Association for the Evaluation of Educational Achievement (IEA).

United Nations Commission on Science and Technology for Development (UNCSTD). 2001. *Knowledge Societies: Information Technology for Sustainable Development*. Oxford: Oxford University Press.

UNESCO (United Nations Educational, Scientific, and Cultural Organization). *Education for All Year 2000 Assessment: Statistical Document*. Paris.

_____. 2001. *Teacher Training through Distance Learning: Technology, Curriculum, Cost, Evaluation: Summary of Case Studies*. Paris.

UNESCO and COMNET-IT (Commonwealth Network of Information Technology for Development Foundation). 2002. *Country Profiles of E-Governance*. Paris.

Urdan, Trace A., and Cornelia C. Weggen. 2000. "Corporate E-Learning: Exploring a New Frontier." San Francisco: WR Hambrecht.

Van Driel, Jan H., William R. Veal, and Fred. J. M. Janssen. 2001. "Pedagogical Content Knowledge: An Integrative Component within the Knowledge Base for Teaching." *Teaching and Teacher Education* 17 (8): 979–986.

Vawda, Ayesha, and Harry Anthony Patrinos. Forthcoming. "Private Education in West Africa: The Technological Imperative." *Journal of Educational Planning and Administration*.

Venezky, Richard L., and Cassandra Davis. 2002. "Quo Vademus? The Transformation of Schooling in a Networked World." Version 8c. OECD Centre for Educational Research and Innovation, Paris. (www.oecd.org/pdf/M00027000/M00027107.pdf)

Venniker, R. 2000. "Social Returns to Education: A Survey of Recent Literature on Human Capital Externalities." CPB Netherlands Bureau for Economic Policy Analysis Report 00/1. The Hague.

Vishwanath, Tara, and Ambar Narayan. 2001. "Informal Economy: Safety Valve or Growth Opportunity?" In Richard Gerster, ed., "Linking Work, Skills, and Knowledge: Learning for Survival and Growth." Swiss Agency for Development and Cooperation (SDC), Berne. (http://www.workandskills.ch/downloads/ConferenceReportWS.pdf)

Walker, David, and Gajaraj Dhanarajan. 2000. "Education for All: The Mass Media Formula." Vancouver: Commonwealth of Learning. (www.col.org/speeches/00efa.htm).

Wang, F.-Y., and A. Mody. 1997. "Explaining Industrial Growth in Coastal China: Economic Reforms . . . and What Else?" *World Bank Economic Review* 11 (2): 293–325.

Weinberg, B.A. 2000. "Computer Use and the Demand for Women Workers." *Industrial and Labor Relations Review* 53 (2): 290–308.

Weir, Sharada. 1999. "The Effects of Education on Farmer Productivity in Rural Ethiopia." Working Paper WPS/99.7. Oxford University, Department of Economics, Centre for the Study of African Economies, United Kingdom.

Welch, F. 1970. "Education in Production." *Journal of Political Economy* 78 (1): 35–59.

Wenglinsky, H. 1998. "Does It Compute? The Relationship between Educational Technology and Student Achievement in Mathematics." Educational Testing Service Policy Information Report. Educational Testing Service, Princeton, New Jersey.

_____. 2000. "How Teaching Matters: Bringing the Classroom Back into Discussions of Teacher Quality." Educational Testing Service, Princeton, New Jersey.

West, Anne, Jo Sparkes, and Todor Balabanov. 2000. "Demand-Side Financing: A Focus on Vouchers in Post-Compulsory Education and Training: Discussion and Case Studies." European Centre for the Development of Vocational Training (CEDEFOP). Thessaloniki, Greece. (http://www2.trainingvillage.gr/etv/publication/download/panorama/6003_en.pdf)

White, B.Y., and J.R. Fredrickson. 1997. *The ThinkerTools Inquiry Project: Making Scientific Inquiry Accessible to Students.* Princeton, N.J.: Center for Performance Assessment, Educational Testing Service.

Winter-Ebmer, R. 1994. "Endogenous Growth, Human Capital, and Industry Wages." *Bulletin of Economic Research* 46 (4): 289–314.

Woessmann, Ludger. 2001. "Schooling Resources, Educational Institutions, and Student Performance: The International Evidence." Kiel Institute for World Economics, Kiel, Germany.

Wolfe, B., and R. Haveman. 2001. "Accounting for the Social and Non-Market Benefits of Education." In J. Helliwell, ed., *The Contribution of Human and Social Capital to Sustained Economic Growth and Well Being.* Paris: OECD.

Wolff, E.N. 2000. "Human Capital Investment and Economic Growth: Exploring the Cross-Country Evidence." *Structural Change and Economic Dynamics* 11 (4): 433–472.

Wood, Adrian. 1994. *North-South Trade, Employment and Inequality: Changing Fortunes in a Skill-Driven World.* Oxford: Clarendon Press.

World Bank. 1991a. "Hungary Human Resources Project." Staff Appraisal Report No. 9183-HU. Europe and Central Asia Region, Human Development Sector Unit, Washington, D.C.

_____. 1991b. *Vocational and Technical Education and Training.* Washington, D.C.

_____. 1994. *Higher Education: The Lessons of Experience.* Washington, D.C.

_____. 1995. *Priorities and Strategies for Education: A World Bank Review.* Washington, D.C.

_____. 1996. "Romania: Reform of Higher Education and Research Project." Staff Appraisal Report No. 15525. Europe and Central Asia Region, Human Development Sector, Washington, D.C.

_____. 1997. *World Development Report.* Washington, D.C.

_____. 1998a. "Attracting High-Technology Investment: Intel's Costa Rican Plant." Human Development Network, Education Group, Washington, D.C.

_____. 1998b. *Education and Training in the East Asia and Pacific Region.* Washington, D.C.

_____. 1998c. "Hungary Human Resources Development Project." Implementation Completion Report No. 17584. Europe and Central Asia Region, Human Development Sector Unit, Washington, D.C.

_____. 1998d. *World Development Report.* Washington, D.C.

_____. 1998e. *Latin America and the Caribbean: Education and Technology at the Crossroads.* Washington, D.C.

_____. 1998f. "Mexico Higher Education Financing Project." Staff Appraisal Report No. 17174. Latin America and the Caribbean Region, Human Development Sector, Washington, D.C.

_____. 1998g. "Venezuela: Stylized Facts and the Characteristics of the Labor Supply in Venezuela: What Can Be Done to Improve the Outcome?" Report 17901-VE. Latin America and Caribbean Region, Human Development Unit, Washington, D.C.

_____. 1999a. *Education in the Middle East and North Africa: A Strategy Towards Learning for Development.* Washington, D.C.

_____. 1999b. *Education Sector Strategy.* Washington, D.C.

_____. 1999c. *Educational Change in Latin America and the Caribbean.* Washington, D.C.

_____. 1999d. "A Proposal for a Comprehensive Development Framework." Washington, D.C.

_____. 2000a. *Hidden Challenges to Education Systems in Transition Economies.* Washington, D.C.

_____. 2000b. *Reforming Public Institutions and Strengthening Governance.* Washington, D.C.

_____. 2000c. *World Development Report.* Washington, D.C.

_____. 2001a. *Brazil: An Assessment of the Bolsa Escola Programs.* Latin America and Caribbean Regional Office, Washington, D.C.

_____. 2001b. *Brazil: The New Growth Agenda.* Latin America and Caribbean Region, Washington, D.C.

_____. 2001c. *Brazil: Secondary Education Profile.* Human Development Network, Education Group, Washington, D.C.

_____. 2001d. *A Chance to Learn: Knowledge and Finance for Education in Sub-Saharan Africa.* Washington, D.C.

_____. 2001e. *Distance Education and Information and Communication Technologies for Learning in Africa.* Africa Region Human Development Working Paper Series, Washington, D.C.

_____. 2001f. *Engendering Development through Gender Equality in Rights, Resources, and Voice.* Washington, D.C.

_____. 2001g. "Jamaica ROSE II Project." Project Appraisal Document No. 10745. Latin America and the Caribbean Region, Human Development Sector, Washington, D.C.

_____. 2001h. *Social Protection Sector Strategy: From Safety Net to Springboard.* Washington, D.C.

_____. 2001i. *World Development Indicators 2001.* Washington, D.C.

_____. 2002a. "Achieving Education for All by 2015: Simulation Results for 47 Low-Income Countries." Human Development Network, Education Group, Washington, D.C. Processed.

_____. 2002b. "Chile Lifelong Learning and Training Project." Project Appraisal Document No. 23632. Latin America and the Caribbean Region, Human Development Sector, Washington, D.C.

_____. 2002c. *Constructing Knowledge Societies: New Challenges for Tertiary Education.* Washington, D.C.

_____. 2002d. *From Natural Resources to the Knowledge Economy: Trade and Job Quality.* Washington, D.C.

_____. 2002e. *Globalization, Growth, and Poverty: Building an Inclusive World Economy.* Washington, D.C.

_____. 2002f. *Information and Communication Technologies.* Washington, D.C.

_____. 2002g. *Rural Strategy: Reaching the Rural Poor.* Washington, D.C.

_____. 2002h. "World Bank Strategy for Science and Technology in Development." Washington, D.C. Processed.

_____. 2002i. *World Development Indicators 2002.* Washington, D.C.

World Bank and IADB (Inter-American Development Bank). 2000. *Secondary Education in Brazil: A Time to Move Forward.* Washington, D.C.

World Bank Institute. 2001a. *China and the Knowledge Economy: Seizing the 21st Century.* Washington, D.C.

_____. 2001b. *Decentralizing Education in Transition Societies: Case Studies from Central Eastern Europe.* Washington, D.C.

_____. 2001c. *Korea and the Knowledge-Based Economy.* Washington, D.C.

WTO (World Trade Organization). 1998. "Education Services." Background note by the Secretariat, S/C/W/49, 98-3691. Geneva.

Yoon, Yangro. 2002. "Effectiveness Born out of Necessity: A Comparison of Korean and East African Education Policies." World Bank, Eastern Europe and Central Asia Region, Washington, D.C.

Ziderman, Adrian. 2001. "Financing Vocational Training to Meet Policy Objectives: Sub-Saharan Africa." World Bank, Africa Region, Human Development Department, Washington, D.C.

Index